Weather of the Heart

Gigi Graham Tchividjian

Weather of the Heart

Glimpses of God in Sunlight and Storm

MULTNOMAH

Portland, Oregon

Unless otherwise indicated, all Scripture references are from the Holy Bible: New International Version, copyright 1973, 1978, 1984 by the International Bible Society. Used by permission of Zondervan Bible Publishers.

Scripture references marked KJV are from the Holy Bible: Authorized King James Version.

Scripture references marked NASB are from the New American Standard Bible, copyright The Lockman Foundation, 1960, 1962, 1963, 1968, 1971, 1972, 1973, 1975, 1977. Used by permission.

Scripture references marked TLB are from The Living Bible, copyright 1971 by Tyndale House Publishers, Wheaton, Ill. Used by permission.

Scripture references marked Amplified are from The Amplified New Testament, copyright 1954, 1958 by The Lockman Foundation. Used by permission.

Scripture references marked Phillips are from J. B. Phillips: The New Testament in Modern English, revised edition, copyright J. B. Phillips 1958, 1960, 1972. Used by permission of Macmillan Publishing Co., Inc.

Portions of this publication previously appeared in Sincerely Gigi, published by Zondervan

Edited by Larry R. Libby
Cover design by Bruce De Roos
Author photo by: Mark Zier, Coral Springs, Fla.

WEATHER OF THE HEART
© 1991 by Gigi Graham Tchividjian
Published by Multnomah Press
10209 SE Division Street
Portland, Oregon 97266

Multnomah Press is a ministry of Multnomah School of the Bible,
8435 NE Glisan Street, Portland, Oregon 97220.

Printed in the United States of America.

Library of Congress Cataloging-in-Publication Data

91 92 93 94 95 96 97 98 99 - 10 9 8 7 6 5 4 3 2 1

Dedication

To Stephan . . .

for helping me discover God in my everyday life.
And for encouraging and challenging me to grow.

My grateful heart belongs to you.

In Appreciation

One day Steve Griffith, Brenda Jose, Larry Libby, and John Van Diest came to my home. Because of Steve's hard work, Brenda's enthusiasm, Larry's sensitive editing skills, and John's OK, this book has become a reality.

A special "thank you" to each one!

Do you think the duck wobbling behind me could have been a dove in disguise?

Also, a very personal note of appreciation to Les Troyer, who never fails to encourage me and to pray for me. Without these, I doubt I could have persevered.

ontents

Part One
Partly Cloudy

The Words We Long to Hear   19

Finding Meaning in the Mundane   23

Summer Survival   27

The Band   31

On Display   37

In a Little White Room   39

Goodbye Again   41

Am I Going to Heaven?   45

Weight of Winter   49

Look Up   53

Above the Fog   55

The Problem   57

You Don't Have to Be Perfect   61

The Burr   63

Am I Appetizing?   67

But How? How? How?   71

Part Two
Storm Watch

The Lesson of the Leaves   77

Fruitful Frustration   81

The Sudden Storm   85

The Defense   89

Beyond the Storm   93

Hope   97

The Day the Sandman Came   103

The Argument   107

But I Don't Have It All Together!   111

The Vase   113

The Plaques   115

"My Heart Is Too Small"   119

The Battlefield   123

The Gentle Touch   127

The Never-Failing Source   131

One of Those Days   135

Unchecked Emotion   139

Failure Isn't Final   143

The Revelation   147

Part Three
Clear Skies

The Tree   153

"Mothers Together"   157

Remembering   161

My Father Loves Me   165

The Example   169

Most Important of All   175

The Same Spirit Says the Same Thing 177

He Is Coming!   181

The Devil's Calling Card   185

Missing Pieces   189

Missing the Splendor   191

Does God Like Me?   195

The Valley   199

A Bunch of Busyness   203

Part Four
Into the Wind

The Reference Point 209

The Letter 213

Devotions or Disaster? 217

How Do You Find the Time? 223

Pass It On 229

The Devil Is a Good Devil 231

I Remember a September Day 235

It Mattered Less Than Love 237

The Green Ribbon 239

The Kiss 241

The Rock 245

Holy Audacity 247

Too Loved to Leave 249

"I'll Be Dogged If I Will" 251

Even This 253

One Step at a Time 255

The Clearing 259

The Place of Refreshment 263

The Disappointment 267

Are You Free? 271

Help! Lord! I Need Strength! 273

Introduction

I lay in the sun watching the children in the pool. *What an ideal lifestyle*, I thought.

We had recently moved to South Florida from the Midwest. What a contrast!

We came from weather that was mostly cloudy and cold, and now it was day after day of sunshine and warmth. After years of living with varying climates . . . the heavy snows of the Swiss Alps, the arid desert land of the Middle East, the drizzle of fall in the Normandy countryside of France, the long, slow months of a Midwest winter, the Lord in His providence chose to place us in this glorious climate.

Suddenly a large, dark thundercloud appeared overhead, blocking the sun's rays. A loud thunderclap caused the children and me to run for cover. I could hear the thunder and see the bright streaks of lightning as I went to my room to change from my swimsuit into jeans in preparation for a rainy afternoon. I emerged a few minutes later only to discover the sun was out again!

The storm had rolled in, bathing our yard in torrential rain, and had left just as quickly. I was so surprised. "Up

North" the rain would probably have continued for hours, if not days. Here it was over before I knew it. These sudden changes in our Florida climate continue to amaze me. I have seen it pour rain in my back yard and walk around to the front yard and find the sun shining brightly. Or, there may be a downpour on one side of the street and bright sunshine on the other.

These sudden changes often remind me of my inner self. My emotions often resemble those weather vanes you see on the rooftops of barns—changing directions with the slightest breeze.

There are the days when I am basking in the sunshine of joy when suddenly a thundercloud of anxiety appears and the tension of the storm quickly replaces the peace.

There are times when clouds of negativism hang over me; their constant dripping cause dreariness of soul and spirit.

There are other days when I feel His wind beneath my wings and I soar with enthusiastic courage, and tackle the challenges of my life with determination and faith.

There are also serene sunny days. Golden days that are free and clear of storms. Days that shine bright and steady with joy and fun and laughter.

I used to be upset, even ashamed of these changing emotions. I thought that a deeply spiritual person should not and would not have these fluctuations of mood. We usually think that women are more prone to emotional currents than men, but when I began to look in Scripture for evidence of mood swings, I found many of the male writers subject to emotional ups and downs. In the psalms, especially, we witness these variations. David is so real and honest about his feelings. One minute he is down and defeated, the next lauding and extolling his Lord. The apostles Peter and Paul, Isaiah, and even the Lord Jesus

Himself (remember that He was touched in every way as we are) all share with us their emotions.

I also began to notice how my spiritual life was affected by the emotional changes in my life. I discovered that when the storm clouds hang low over me and the fog rolls in thick around me and the constant drizzle of discouragement dismays me, that my spiritual life tends to blossom.

I do love sunshine, but as an old Arab proverb says, "All sunshine makes a desert."

So, He gives me enough sunshine to keep me healthy and happy and enough clouds and rain to keep me nourished and fertile and totally dependent upon Him.

The meditations on the following pages have been arranged according to mood or "weather" rather than any attempt at a chronological order. They span the days of my life—from my childhood home in the mountains of North Carolina to the glorious Alps where Stephan and I lived as newlyweds to recent days in balmy South Florida. As you read and ponder. I pray that you will be encouraged to not only endure your changing emotions, but to come to appreciate and cherish the "weather of your heart."

Part One
Partly Cloudy

Do you know how God controls the clouds? . . .
Do you know how the clouds hang poised,
those wonders of him who is perfect in knowledge?
Job 37: 15,16

The Words
We Long to Hear

I sat with my seventeen-year-old son in the driver's license bureau. We had been waiting for forty-five minutes just to have our number called.

A "no smoking" sign hung prominently from the ceiling, but the man behind me had decided to ignore it. I looked around the room at the stiff plastic seats, the florescent lights, and the dirty white walls.

Why do government offices all look and feel the same? I asked myself.

Every few minutes, a bureaucratic voice—sounding halfway between a grumble and a scolding—would call out the next number.

When our number was finally called, my seventeen-year-old son and I jumped up and hurried to the counter. We were told to sit down again and wait.

After what seemed like another hour, we heard our name again. The woman at the counter smiled at my son and then turned to me.

"Is he yours?" she asked.

"Yes," I replied. "One of seven."

"You are lovely," she said with a smile.

I couldn't believe it. I was hot, tired, and wilted, feeling anything but lovely. I thanked her and returned to my seat. As this woman assisted my son, I overheard her say, "Your mother is beautiful. You must be so proud of her."

Suddenly that dreary, boring bureau became bright and cheery. My spirits lifted. I forgot the monotonous wait and felt good all over. Encouraged!

Isn't it strange how much easier it is to do the dishes when the children tell you they really enjoyed the meal? Or how the cleaning doesn't seem so much like drudgery when your husband remarks that the house looks nice?

My husband, Stephan, tells me it is much easier to get up day after day and go to work when he knows his family appreciates all he does. I have seen his tired face change and his eyes light up when I remember to express my gratitude.

Encouragement is a key to success in any relationship. This is especially true within the family, because it builds emotional security and self-esteem.

But what exactly is encouragement? We usually think of it as "praise." And while praise is certainly an important ingredient, there is more to encouragement than admiration and applause.

Encouragement is being a good listener.

As a busy mother, I often find I don't put much effort into listening to my family. When I think of the encouragers in my life, my maternal grandmother would be high on the list. Not only did she take time to listen, but she

always looked for the good qualities in each one of her grandchildren . . . and was slow to condemn.

Encouragement is being positive.

It is recognizing effort and *improvement.* Just as it is important to speak up at the appropriate time, it is also important to know when *not* to speak. I tend to point out the faults of my children more often than I recognize their honest efforts to improve.

Encouragement is letting others know you accept them for who they are.

I know one father who says he cannot love his children unless they please him. His acceptance is based on their *performance.* How thankful I am that my heavenly Father's acceptance is based on love through the sacrifice of His Son, not on my track record.

Encouragement is offering hope.

The prophet prompts us to speak a word in season to the weary (Isaiah 50:4). My psychologist husband tells me the saddest cases he sees in his office are those who have lost hope.

Encouragement is caring about the feelings of another.

Understanding is a vital part of encouragement. I found a card recently that read: "I can't say that I know how you feel, because I don't. But I can say that I care, because I do." That's encouragement.

How can we become encouragers?

First of all, by letting it become a habit! Look for every opportunity to practice encouragement, speaking words of praise. Avoid placing blame as much as possible. Be positive. Read Philippians 4:8 and put it into practice.

Try to understand how the other person feels. My mother suggests that one way to accomplish this is by spending a few minutes praying every day for the specific needs of others.

Then . . . pause to think how the Lord encourages *you*.

We had just spent a delightful weekend with our daughter who lives in Orlando. As we climbed into the van for the long drive home, I felt depressed. I was sad to leave Berdjette, and was dreading all the work and responsibility of the upcoming week.

As each mile took me farther from my daughter and closer to my busy week, I felt more discouraged. Soon the palm trees faded from view as twilight turned to darkness—reflecting my inner feelings. The children in the back seat—busy with their games and petty arguments—were oblivious to my despondency.

But the Lord knew.

Suddenly, from the darkness behind me, a strong, clear, six-year-old voice began to sing,

"My God is so big, so strong, and so mighty,
There's nothing my God cannot do.
The mountains are His, the valleys are His,
The stars are His handiwork, too.
My God is so big, so strong, and so mighty,
There's nothing my God cannot do . . . *for you!*"

Tears of gratitude flooded my eyes.

Thank You, Lord, for encouraging me.

Finding Meaning
in the Mundane

I slowly pulled myself out of the soft couch where I had plopped after putting the youngest to bed. I picked up each cushion and puffed it back into shape. With each "puff," I wondered to myself just how many times I had done this before.

I collected the various cups, glasses, and mugs lying around, turned off the lights, and walked into the kitchen. I filled the coffee maker for the next morning, making sure the timer was set for 6:00 A.M., wiped the counters, turned on the dishwasher, checked the dog's water, and locked the front door.

As I walked to my room, I noticed the dirty clothes basket. Full. Again. I passed the children's bathroom and saw wet towels strewn around the floor, tangled with assorted sneakers and a stray pair of dirty socks. With a sigh, I hung up the towels and picked up the shoes.

I was tired. It was hard to keep back the tears of frustration and discouragement.

Lying in bed, I thought back on my day. *What in the world have I accomplished?*

—Swept up dog hair and cookie crumbs.
—Washed and ironed several loads of wash.
—Washed windows—that were immediately
  smeared with sticky fingerprints.
—Chauffeured children.
—Shopped for groceries.
—Prepared dinner.
—Recleaned kitchen.
—Repuffed couch pillows.
—Set timer on coffee pot.

And what did I have to look forward to tomorrow? *More of the same.*

I looked over at my sleeping husband. He was not immune to the tedium, either. He too must struggle at times with the monotony of the mundane. Each morning he rises before 6:00 to be on time at his office. He follows the same daily routine and works long, hard hours to support his large family. He never complains, and yet, I am sure he too often feels frustrated and discouraged at the end of the day.

I thought of how much our lives are . . . well . . . so *daily*. How often our hours are filled with the mundane, seemingly unimportant things that have to be done, whether at home or work.

Recently our eldest daughter Berdjette came for a visit. As we stood in the kitchen washing dishes, one of the younger children needed to be disciplined. Berdjette observed me doing the same things I had been doing twenty odd years before when she was a small child.

She smiled and shook her head. "Mama, you've been doing *this* for such a long time now."

24

As I lay there in the darkness, fighting back tears, I realized I was in danger (once again) of becoming encumbered and defeated by the mundane.

Satan would like nothing better than to discourage us as marriage partners and parents. He would like nothing better than to have us so burdened by the everyday details of life that we forget the blessings. To cause us to feel insignificant and to make us believe our efforts are of little importance in "the great scheme of things."

Oh Lord, I prayed, *show me again how to look at my tasks and responsibilities from Your perspective.*

And late into the silence of that night, He did just that.

My thoughts drifted back to a time when Stephan and I lived in the Middle East. We didn't have all of the modern conveniences I had been accustomed to. So we made do. I didn't have a washer or dryer, so each morning I placed a large pot of water on the stove to boil. I put all the baby's diapers in this pot, then rinsed them and hung them on the line to dry. I washed the sheets, towels, and clothing in the bathtub and would ask Stephan to help me wring out the larger items.

A visiting friend returned home and related our situation to my mother. I'll never forget Mother's next letter. She expressed her concern for me and the responsibilities I carried, but then added, "I am so thankful that you have clothes to wash and hands and soap with which to wash them."

Thankfulness. This is not only God's perspective, it is His will for us. Through the apostle, He tells us, "Be thankful," and "give thanks in all circumstances, for this is God's will for you in Christ Jesus" (Colossians 3:15; 1 Thessalonians 5:18).

As I lay in the comfort of my bed, still unable to sleep, I remembered a recent trip to a Third World country.

I visualized the tired, overburdened women squatting alongside riverbanks, washing their simple, tattered clothing in muddy water. Each morning these women cooked their meager meals over fires of wood. How grateful I am to have a washing machine. How thankful that we have clothes to wash, bathrooms to straighten and scrub, plentiful food to cook, and a kitchen to clean. How thankful that my husband has a job to go to each day and that we have a home to come back to each evening.

The more I thought of my blessings, the less discouraged I felt. Satan had caused my negative attitude to so quickly overshadow God's bountiful provisions.

Quietly, in the depths of that night, the Lord reminded me that *serving* is the highest of callings. That He Himself came to serve, not to be served (Matthew 23:11; Mark 10:44-45).

He never asked us to be successes by society's standards.

He said with great solemnity, "I tell you the truth, whatever you did for one of the least of these . . . you did for me" (Matthew 25:40).

Then aren't we obeying Him and following His calling and example when we serve our families?

By doing all of the small, mundane tasks required in a family, even hanging up wet towels and picking up dirty socks, aren't we really serving Him?

I silently offered my routine days and mundane responsibilities as a sacrifice to Him. These very "daily" tasks could become a celebration of praise and adoration.

"It is through consecration," someone has said, "that drudgery is made divine."

I fell asleep, eager to begin tomorrow.

Summer Survival

I made my way slowly down the narrow, winding, dirt road. The lush mountain undergrowth brushed up against the van as I cautiously hugged my side of the road around each curve. I felt a certain sense of frivolous freedom. I had just deposited three of my children in summer camp.

A whole week to myself! Almost. Number seven was still too young for camp.

Each year, as summer approaches, I have mixed emotions. I enjoy being with the children and having a more relaxed schedule, but after a few days, I quickly realize that school is not so much for children as it is for parents.

I soon become frustrated by a permanently disorderly house. Rooms I just straightened are a mess in minutes. The newspaper I just picked up is dumped carelessly on the floor, the sports pages spread out like a carpet. Damp Fruity Pebbles cling to what had been a clean kitchen table. Paper cups, popsicle sticks, and wet towels seem to sprout from one end of the yard to the other, and I weary of yelling hundreds of times a day, "Close the door! The air conditioner is on and we are *not* cooling all of Coral Springs, Florida."

I loath the countless, foolish arguments that require me, the resident judge, to settle. I tire of being social director for children whose imaginations seem so limited. I grind my teeth in frustration when the dishes have just been washed and put away—and everyone comes trooping back into the kitchen for a snack. For three months, I, along with thousands of parents, try to discover creative ways to survive the summer.

One day, when I was feeling particularly frazzled, I looked up the word "weary" in Webster's dictionary. The definition read: "Worn out in strength, endurance, vigor, or freshness. Having one's patience, tolerance, or pleasure exhausted."

I had to chuckle. It sounded as if Webster were describing a parent.

There are no easy solutions to summer survival . . . unless you are one of the few who send all the children to camp all summer. If you are, then you need read no further.

I have been "surviving" summers for over twenty-seven years now. Although I have three grown children who are "on their own" at this writing, I still have four, including the one who is too young for camp, and three grandchildren, who keep me challenged during the summer. And I've learned a few helpful hints along the way. . . .

Cultivate a Positive Attitude

William James, the great American psychologist, said, "The greatest discovery of my generation is that people can alter their lives by altering their attitudes."

I have found this to be true. If I approach summertime

with dread, it will be dreadful. However, if I anticipate enjoyment, chances are it will be enjoyable.

Yes, there will be harried, hectic days. But there will also be precious time with the children that will never be recaptured.

Throttle Down

When the days become long, hot, and humid, and my nerves fray because the children are under foot all day, I try to remember to take a deep breath and relax.

I sort of put myself in neutral. I plan not to have any firm, fixed plans. I try to eliminate as many deadlines and demands as possible. I find that if I am under constant pressure it is difficult to have pleasure. When interruptions begin to interrupt my interruptions, I become increasingly irritable. Soon, the things in my life which are really blessings become more like burdens. So, since I have learned that summer will be hectic, I now try to allow for it.

Plan for Pleasure

One way that I anticipate enjoyment is to plan for it.

I plan to enjoy my children. We do things together. When we are at home in Florida, we go to the beach, have cookouts, work in the yard, or get together with friends. When we are in the mountains of North Carolina, we plan outings. An afternoon hike up a mountain, a picnic by the stream, or a leisurely evening walk. On rainy days we go to a movie or sit by the fire and roast marshmallows. I ask the Lord to help me think of simple ways to build happy memories for my family.

Take Advantage of Small Snatches

In a hectic household, I have learned to take advantage of small snatches of time. Whether it be for personal pleasure,

physical rest, or spiritual refreshment, small moments of time can provide the desired relief that we all require.

Reading and meditating on just one verse of Scripture can provide spiritual refreshment all throughout the day. Taking time to enjoy simple pleasures, like the smell of fresh-mowed grass, or the soft balmy breezes blowing across your face, or the rain drops lingering on a leaf after a sudden thunderstorm, or perhaps sitting for a few moments in your favorite chair listening to soft music after the kids are in bed all offer mental and physical relief in a frenzied day.

Evaluate Priorities

I also find that summer is a good time to reevaluate my priorities. I try to be honest with myself, and ask, "Which is more important, the muddy footprints, or the small feet that made them?" Often I have to admit that having my floor clean and my house straight has become too important. I'm inclined to make an issue of little things instead of remembering that "this too shall pass."

So I work hard at lowering my expectations. The children's rooms will not stay neat. The clothes will not be hung up. The windows will have fingerprints. The floor will be sandy. The door will be left open. There will be arguments to settle, and snacks to fix. Paper cups will still have to be picked up and on certain days I will feel as if I am living on the edge of a scream.

But suddenly, it is September again. The alarm awakens me to the first day of a new school year. As I drive home from depositing the children in their various classrooms, the van seems eerily quiet. I open the front door to a calm, clean house that will stay that way until four o'clock. With a tinge of regret that the holidays have so quickly faded into fall, I bow my head and thank the Lord that I survived another summer.

The Band

I pulled myself out of bed earlier than usual to drive my sister to the hospital, some fifteen miles away, for minor surgery. The sunrise whispered hints of a glorious day to come . . . but I couldn't take time to listen.

I returned home and mechanically ran through my routine: straightening, cleaning, laundry. With the house in some semblance of order, I made the round-robin circuit of grocery store, bank, and cleaners. I made it back just in time to put away groceries, fold laundry, and set the table for dinner—before rushing back to the hospital to pick up my sister.

After getting her settled in the guest room, I quickly began to throw something together for supper. Soon I heard the children arriving home from school. They threw down their books, grabbed a snack, and headed off down the hall. A little later, an argument erupted outside in the yard. I went to investigate, and sure enough, the youngest was baiting the older ones and they were reacting as he had hoped they would.

I sighed as I went out the door to mediate. *What do my poor neighbors think?* I suddenly remembered a sign in a hotel lobby: "Sorry for the noise and confusion, but we are growing." I wished I had two of these signs, one for the front yard and another for the back. I called the children to come and eat. After rushing them through dinner and into some clean clothes, we piled into the car. It was the night of Jerushah's junior high band concert.

As we raced along the road, I noticed the sun setting over the Everglades, lighting the western sky with rose-colored fire. I realized I hadn't taken time to enjoy even one minute of the day's beauty.

I deposited Jerushah at the appointed place—a few minutes late—and with the other children in tow, filed into the sanctuary of the church where the concert was to be held.

Exhausted, I plopped into the nearest empty pew, hoping I wouldn't have to speak to anyone. Although parents and children were talking and laughing, the cool stone walls, soft red carpet, and deep polished wood all offered a hint of serenity to my tired body and spirit.

Then the members of the band streamed in and began to tune their instruments. And all sense of calm went out the back door.

Each instrument sounded out of tune and off key. My already-frayed nerves unraveled a little further.

I watched the musicians. Some seemed enthusiastic and gave serious attention to tuning their instruments. Others couldn't have cared less, and seemed oblivious to the importance of the occasion. Some, especially the boys, gave the distinct impression they wished to be anywhere but here.

Everything seemed out of tune. Out of sync.

They blew, tooted, tweeted, squawked, whacked, and plucked until I wondered which would explode first, my ears or my nerves.

Perfect. I told myself. *A perfect ending to a frazzled day.*

I longed for home. And bed. And quiet.

Suddenly the director walked in.

She stood quietly erect, in control, in command. Within seconds, every student was looking directly at her. Her eyes held them at attention. Then she lifted her arms and began to direct.

Amazingly, a recognizable tune emerged from the previous chaos. As I listened, I was surprised to discover they weren't bad at all. I relaxed—a little—and began to enjoy the concert I had dreaded.

As one tune flowed smoothly into another, I began to realize that with a good director, discipline, encouragement, and a lot of practice and patience, even the smallest band could make a joyful noise to the Lord.

I thought of how many similarities this band had to my life and family. Can you imagine just how awful we must sound to the One who created precision, order, and harmony in the universe? In God's ears we must all sound out of tune.

I winced, thinking of the disharmony of my hectic day. The rushing, the screaming, the traffic, the constant ringing of the telephone, the noise and confusion of just getting the family through a "normal" day.

How often our days must grate on His holy ears.

I watched the attractive, erect director. With all her knowledge and training, that small junior high band must

often strain her musical sensibilities. Yet she patiently encouraged, inspired, and assured her students. Although demanding discipline, practice, and strict attention, she also made it obvious that each member was important. When one got off key or out of sync, she didn't scold unfairly, or embarrass unnecessarily, she just had another cover for him.

What a good example for me as a parent. My little band seems so out of tune and off key at times that "my nerves are screaming thin and bare for all the world to see."

Yet, when I get out of tune or off key, the Lord is so patient with me. So encouraging. He doesn't scold or berate. He even sends others to cover for me. A note of encouragement . . . a friend calling to say she is praying . . . or maybe even Stephan offering to take us all out for pizza when I'm too tired to cook.

This director did not expect her students to perform like the Philharmonic . . . but only to give their best. And the Lord does not demand perfection from me. He doesn't expect more from me than I am capable of giving. So I should be with my children.

As director/mom, I need to be in control, encourage discipline, and command respect and attention. But I must also be patient, offering encouragement and assurance of each child's individual worth. In order to do this effectively, it is imperative for me to keep my eyes on the Director, to follow His lead, to heed His instructions.

I'm so glad David chose the word "noise" and not "perfect harmony" when he said, "Make a joyful noise unto God" (Psalm 66:1, KJV). We are not capable of perfection; we will make mistakes and hit many false notes before this life is through. But the Lord doesn't give up on us, and we don't have to achieve perfection before He can use us.

Through His loving direction and our faithful perse-

vering we will be conformed more and more to His image. One day we will not only make a joyful noise, but be presented faultless, in perfect harmony, to the Father.

On Display

"**G**igi! Anne! Bunny! Franklin!" they called to the four Graham children. Ned had not yet been born.

It was Sunday afternoon and once again the tourists had arrived. They came by the busload from the nearby conference centers and streamed into our yard, calling our names in the hope that we would come out and pose for pictures. We hid inside behind closed doors and pulled drapes, peeking out every now and then to watch as they chipped wood from our little rail fence and snapped pictures of our home to take back as souvenirs. As children, we didn't understand all this intrusion and attention. To us, Daddy was just Daddy. But because he was well-known, we children were on display.

In looking back I realize this was just another part of God's training program for my life. As Christians, aren't all of us on display before a watching world? We may not always relish the idea; we may find it at times to be inconvenient or burdensome. But we must always be conscious of the fact that representing Jesus Christ to others is a responsibility and privilege reserved for the children of the King.

May we always be aware that what we *are* speaks so loudly that the world can't hear what we *say*.

In a Little White Room

I loved the little room I shared with my sister Anne. It was white, with a lovely bay window where the rhododendron bushes outside snuggled up so close you could almost reach out and touch their soft pink blossoms. Just beyond, the mountains towered so high we had to lean way down or go outside to see the top of the ridge called "Rainbow."

I slept in a big white bed. It really wasn't very big; it was just that I was so small. We had two closets, one on each side of the room. The closet on the right was special, because high above it—out of reach—was a small cupboard where mother would find special treats. (These were confiscated from birthdays and Christmases when we were inundated with toys, and saved for sick-in-bed days.) Once, when I hurt my finger and had to have stitches, Mother reached in and found a lovely new baby doll for me.

When I was four, I became so ill that even the surprise from the hidden cupboard didn't make me feel any better. Mother was concerned and watched me closely. One day she came into my little room and sat down on the edge of the bed. She lovingly stroked my burning forehead and said, "God loves you very much, Gigi—so much that He sent His Son, Jesus, to die on the cross for you."

Then she repeated once again the story I had heard many times before. She explained how Jesus had been beaten and spit upon, and that although He had done nothing to deserve such treatment, He had taken that cruel punishment for me. He had even been nailed to a cross and left to die, and by taking our sins—our "badness"—on Himself, He was making it possible for us to live with Him forever in heaven when we die. She told me that even if I, Gigi Graham, had been the only little girl in the whole world, God would still have sent His Son to die—just for me.

"Gigi." Mother's voice was very gentle. "If you wish, you could ask Jesus to come into your heart right now."

Oh, how I wanted to do just that! So in simple, childlike faith I opened my heart to Him and He came in—forgiving my "badness. " I certainly didn't understand the theological implications of that moment, nor did I experience much emotionally. But I felt clean . . . and very much loved.

That day long ago, in my little upstairs bedroom, God began something in my life. And He isn't through with me. He continues to shape and mold me, adding His finishing touches.

Have you personally met Jesus Christ? Are you confident of your relationship with Him? He's as near you right now as He was near to me in that little white room in the mountains.

You, too, are very much loved.

Goodbye Again

But one thing I do: Forgetting what is behind
and straining toward what is ahead,
I press on toward the goal.
(Philippians 3:13-14).

Mother stood waiting outside the doorway.

The suitcases were packed and standing in the hallway, ready to be loaded into the car. We children ran around the driveway, laughing and playing while we waited for Daddy. Suddenly his tall, handsome figure appeared in the doorway, overcoat slung over one arm, hat on his head. We ran to him, dreading what we knew would be another long separation. He took each of us in his strong arms, held us tightly, and then kissed us goodbye.

I couldn't bear to look into his eyes, because I knew they would be glistening with tears. Though there were many such goodbyes while we were growing up, it never got easier. We backed away and watched as Daddy took mother in his arms, kissing her warmly and firmly, knowing it would be some time before he would hold her again.

Then before we knew it, Daddy was whisked away in the car, around the curves and down the steep mountain drive. We listened to the retreating sound of the engine and waited for the final "toot" of the horn as he reached the gate. Another plane to catch, another city, another crusade, another period of weeks before we would be together as a family once more.

I turned to look at Mother, sensing her feeling of loss and loneliness. Her eyes were bright with unshed tears, but there was a beautiful smile on her face as she said, "Okay, let's clean the attic! Then we'll have LaoNaing and Lao I up for supper!" (Chinese for maternal grandmother and maternal grandfather. Mother's parents, the Nelson Bells, served for twenty-five years as missionaries to China. They retired to a home only a mile down the mountain from us.)

Not once did my mother ever make us feel that by staying behind she was sacrificing her life for us children. By her sweet, positive example, her consistently unselfish spirit, and her total reliance upon the person of Jesus Christ, we were kept from bitterness and resentment. We learned, instead, to look for ways to keep busy and prepare for Daddy's homecoming.

Years later, I asked Mother how she had endured so many years of goodbyes. She laughed and quoted the old mountain man who said, "Make the least of all that goes, and the most of all that comes."

> We live a time
> secure;
> beloved and loving,
> sure
> it cannot last
> for long,
> then—
> the goodbyes come
> again—again—
> like a small death,
> the closing of a door.

One learns to live
with pain.
One looks ahead,
not back—
never back,
only before.
And joy will come again—
warm and secure,
if only for the now,
laughing,
we endure.

Ruth Bell Graham

Mother's example returns to my heart again and again through the years: Don't regret what is past. Cherish what you have. Look forward to all that is to come. And most important of all, rely moment by moment on Jesus Christ.

Am I Going to Heaven?

One Friday afternoon, Mother promised to take Anne, Bunny, and me to our mountain cabin to spend the night.

When we arrived home from school, Mama had everything all packed, and after changing into playclothes, we piled into the Jeep. Soon we were bouncing along the old dirt road that climbed steeply upward to the small one-room cabin.

After a supper of hot dogs and hot chocolate prepared over the open fire, we sat on the porch, reading and talking until dark. Then suddenly I asked a question that had been troubling me all afternoon.

"Mama, if I die, will I go to heaven?"

I had good reason to ask, for that very afternoon, for the umpteenth time, I had been punished for teasing my little sister.

"You tell *me*," she replied.

"I don't know."

"Do you want me to tell you how you can know?"

"I don't think you can know for sure."

"Oh, yes, you can."

"How?"

"First," she explained, "you know that you are a sinner, don't you?"

"Of course!" There was never any doubt about *that*. I always seemed to be getting into trouble.

"Then, you confess your sins to Him."

"I've done that," I nodded. "After I got so mad this afternoon, I told Him I was sorry three times—just in case He didn't hear me the first time."

"He heard you the first time," Mama said. "You are a child of God because you asked Jesus into your heart. Do you remember being born into God's family when you were only four?"

"No," I shook my head. "I don't remember it. I only know what you've told me. And I'm still not sure I'm going to heaven."

"Gigi, just because you can't remember the day doesn't make it any less real." Her voice became stern for a moment. "Would you call God a liar?"

"Of course not!" I protested.

"But that's just what you're doing," she insisted. "He tells us that if we confess, He will forgive (1 John 1:9). If we believe, we have eternal life (1 John 2:25). You have confessed and you believe—yet you don't think God will keep His promise. That's the same as calling Him a liar."

She paused a moment for me to reflect on her words.

"Don't you recall what John 3:16 says? Recite it for me."

I repeated the familiar, much-loved verse: "For God so loved the world, that he gave his only begotten Son that whosoever believeth in him should not perish, but have everlasting life" (KJV).

Then Mama held up a piece of paper and said, "Whoever wants it can have it."

I snatched it from her fingers.

"What makes you think I said *you*?" Mama demanded.

"You said 'whoever.' "

"Exactly."

We knelt beside the cabin's bed and prayed for assurance.

"Mama," I said breathlessly as we rose to our feet, "I feel like a new person."

The next day, this "new person" scampered down Assembly Drive to the Montreat gate and uprooted a dozen water lilies that had just been planted in time for the arrival of the season's first tourists and conferees. Mama escorted me to the town manager's office with the evidence wilting in my tight little fist, my face pale as I worried aloud that I was going to be thrown into jail (Mama saying absolutely nothing to dispel the fear).

I confessed and apologized. With so much practice, I was a good little "repenter."

That night as Mama tucked me into bed, I asked plaintively, "Have I been good enough today to go to heaven?"

"Now, how much," wrote Mama in her diary that night, "should I impress on Gigi the doctrine of salvation by grace when, really, for a child of her disposition, one could be tempted to think that salvation by works would be more effective?"

That was not the last time I was plagued with doubts, because "being good" has been harder for me than for some. The Devil loves to make me feel unworthy of God's love and grace to the point that I even wonder at times if I am really saved.

But the Scriptures clearly teach that His love is unconditional, and that salvation is by grace alone, not dependent on my performance or feelings.

For that, I will be eternally grateful.

Weight of Winter

God of my righteousness:
thou hast enlarged me when I was in distress
(Psalm 4:1, KJV).

The icy wind burned my cheeks, but I stood there as long as I could, watching the retreating figure of the man I loved as he trudged off into the snow to catch his train. I turned to close the door and, suddenly, loneliness engulfed me.

Stephan had been called away for a few weeks of military duty, and I was left with only two infant children for company in this small German-speaking village high in the Swiss Alps, miles away from our own home. Tears stung my eyes as I turned out the lights, gathered the children, and climbed the stairs to bed.

If the nights were long, the days seemed interminable.

Each morning I awoke with the same sinking feeling. After breakfast I would bundle up the children and walk to the village that lay a mile down the winding road. We would buy our groceries, window-shop, occasionally stop at a tearoom for hot chocolate, then walk home. But each

time I entered the old chalet, I felt its unfamiliar walls closing in on me.

I felt abandoned and confined—confined to a small
apartment that was cold and foreign, confined by the
walls of snow outside the windows, confined by the language barrier, confined by the fact that my family and
friends were far away, confined by the small children who
couldn't understand my frustration. I felt pressed on every
side, and it wasn't long before self-pity began to work its
way into my very being, and I was utterly miserable.

One day as I sat alone at the kitchen table complaining to the Lord, it occurred to me that I was missing a perfect opportunity to practice the presence of God and prove
His promises. So each afternoon after the children were
tucked into bed for their naps, I would stoke the fire, fix a
pot of tea, sit down at the antique desk, and spend time
with the Lord. I cried out to Him like Isaiah when he said,
"O LORD, I am oppressed; undertake for me" (Isaiah 38:14,
KJV). And, like David, I poured out my frustration:
"Therefore is my spirit overwhelmed within me; my heart
within me is desolate" (Psalm 143:4, KJV). Then I would
steep myself in His Word, soaking it in, allowing Him to
love me.

Oh, how real He became to me!

True to every promise, He took my burden, lifted me
up, undertook for me, and gave me peace and joy in the
midst of my loneliness. Soon I was able to enjoy the walks
to the village, appreciate the companionship of my children, enjoy the beauty around me—the snow glistening in
the sunlight, the glory of the mountain peaks, the skaters
and skiers in their bright jackets. Before I knew it, it was
time to throw open the door and greet Stephan once again.

Many years have come and gone since that cold,
lonely winter. And looking back, I wouldn't trade that

experience for anything. The misery lasted only a few weeks, but the precious lesson has lasted a lifetime.

My experience was not unique. Everyone has times when they feel confined—by small children, finances, illness, loneliness, circumstances beyond control. But I have discovered:

> If loving hearts were never lonely,
>> If all they wish might
>>> always be
> accepting what they look for only,
>> They might be glad,
>>> but not in Thee.
>>>> A. L. Waring

Look Up

When I am afraid, I will trust in you
(Psalm 56:3).

tephan, the children, and I slowly climbed the steep, narrow road that wound its way up the side of the mountain to our little village high in the Swiss Alps. The sun was sinking lower and lower behind the ridge that loomed up just ahead. We knew it would be only a few more sharp turns in our little car before we would be face-to-face with the dreaded bridge.

As dusk fell, the large evergreens seemed to close in on us, casting ghostly shadows along the road. We never liked crossing the rickety old bridge, especially since caution signs had been posted. But it was the only way to span the deep ravine that separated one side of the valley from the other.

There it was—challenging and taunting us. As we started across, grateful that no other cars were adding their weight, our four-year-old son suddenly cried out in fear. His younger sister looked at him with understanding. Perhaps reassuring herself as much as her brother, she said, "Stephan-Nelson, don't be afraid. Look up—not down."

There have been many times in my own life when I have been afraid.

> Afraid of the unknown.
> Afraid when a child has been very ill.
> Afraid in a lurching airplane on a stormy night.
> Afraid to speak out.
> Afraid to disappoint—or be disappointed.
> Afraid of being found out.
> Afraid of rejection.
> Afraid to take a stand.
> Afraid of losing.
> Afraid of being alone.
> Afraid to make a decision.
> Afraid of pain.

Some of my fears are real; some are imaginary. Some are physical; others, psychological or emotional. Some are for myself and some are for loved ones. Whatever the fear, I have felt it keenly—an unpleasant experience. Invariably, the bridge between despair and hope looks awesome and precarious when I am looking down into myself—my circumstances, my feelings, my emotions—instead of looking up and trusting in Him whom my soul loves.

> "Turn your eyes upon Jesus
> Look full in His wonderful face;
> And the things of earth will grow strangely dim
> In the light of His glory and grace."[1]

We are lifted above our circumstances when we look into the face of Jesus.

Note

1. Helen H. Lemmel, *Turn Your Eyes Upon Jesus*, © 1922, renew © 1950 by H. H. Lemmel assigned to Singsperation.

Above the Fog

*I lift up my eyes to the hills—where does my help
come from? My help comes from the LORD,
the Maker of heaven and earth*
(Psalm 121:1-2).

It was a cold, dreary, foggy day in our little Swiss village. Tired of being indoors, the children begged to go for a ride in the *telecabine* which ran up to one of the mountain peaks directly behind our chalet. I had to admit that it sounded tempting, so leaving the household chores behind, I bundled the little ones in their warm coats and soon we were all snuggled into the tiny cable car.

In only a matter of moments we were suspended high above the ground, moving slowly through the dense fog that engulfed us. Suddenly we broke through the clouds and there, surrounding us, bathed in brilliant sunshine, were the glorious mountain peaks. We stepped out of the little car and onto the terrace where we sat in the sun, soaking up its warmth while we sipped hot chocolate and tried to capture forever the splendor of the moment.

All too soon it was time to return. We descended slowly, and it wasn't long before we were once again enshrouded by the low-hanging clouds and the dreary dampness of the valley fog.

I couldn't help realizing that this experience is often paralleled in my life. I love the mountaintop experiences, the times when I am transported beyond the fog to bask in the warmth of the Son and His love, leaving the dailiness and dreariness behind and feeling only the splendor and majesty of His presence. But often I feel confined to a life of foggy valleys: the mundane, the frustrations, the difficulties of valley life that seem to overwhelm me. And I grow weary of trying to climb out of the fog.

> The hills on which I need to gaze
> are wrapped in clouds again.
> I lift up streaming eyes in vain
> and feel upon my upturned face
> the streaming rain.
>
> Ruth Bell Graham

I long to go up in a little cable car and rise above it all, break out of the fog, see life from a higher perspective. I wish to experience that indescribable feeling of peace, security, power, stability, serenity—all that those mountains represent. Then I begin to catch a glimpse of the obvious. I do have a way out of the fog . . . whenever I choose to pray.

> Lord, when my soul is weary
> and my heart is tired and sore,
> and I have that failing feeling
> that I can't take it any more;
> then let me know the freshening
> found in childlike prayer,
> when the kneeling soul knows surely
> that a listening Lord is there.
>
> Ruth Bell Graham

As the fog descends on the valleys of our lives, may we allow His eternal presence to envelop and protect us.

The Problem

Your attitude should be the same
as that of Christ Jesus
(Philippians 2:5).

I stood in the upstairs hallway, looking down over the bannister, waiting for the younger children to come in for their baths. My oldest daughter, taking a piano lesson, was in the living room directly below, and the repetitive melody she was playing echoed through my mind. Standing there, I savored both the few moments of solitude and the aroma from the roast beef and apple pie already in the oven.

Suddenly the little ones bounded through the door. I cringed as I saw their muddy footprints on the white carpet and their filthy little hands leaving distinct imprints on the cream-colored walls. They bounced up to their rooms, cheeks flushed and eyes bright from their play.

I noticed, however, that one of my young sons was trudging slowly up the stairs, his head bowed, grubby hands covering his small, dirt-streaked face. When he reached the top, I asked him what was wrong.

"Aw, nothing," he replied.

"Then why are you holding your face in your hands?"

"Oh, I was just praying."

Quite curious now, I asked what he was praying about.

"I can't tell you," he insisted, "because if I do, you'll be mad."

After much persuasion I convinced him he could confide in me and that, whatever he told me, I would not get mad. So he explained that he was praying about a problem he had with his mind.

"A problem with your mind?" I asked, now more curious than ever. What kind of problem could a six-year-old have with his mind?

"Well," he said, "you see, every time I pass by the living room, I see my piano teacher, and my tongue sticks out."

Hard as it was to keep a straight face, I took his problem seriously and assured him that God could, indeed, help him with it.

Later, on my knees beside the bathtub as I bathed this little fellow, I thought how I still struggle with the problem of controlling my mind and my tongue. All too often my mind focuses on the negative until negativism dominates my thoughts and actions. I find myself being critical and unpleasant. Repeatedly I realize that I have said what I didn't mean to say, and haven't said what I really wanted to say—such as, "Thank you" or, "Well done!" or even, "I love you." All too often I focus on faults, while ignoring or forgetting the much-needed word of praise, encouragement, or appreciation.

That afternoon as I knelt to scrub that sturdy little body, the tub became my altar; the bathroom, my temple. I

bowed my head, covered my face, and acknowledged that I, like my son, had a problem with my mind and tongue. I asked the Lord to forgive me and to give me more and more the mind and heart of Christ.

> May the mind of Christ my Savior
> Live in me from day to day,
> By His love and power controlling
> All I do and say.
>   Kate B. Wilkinson

You Don't Have to Be Perfect

*I don't mean to say I am perfect. I haven't learned
all that I should even yet, but I keep working toward
that day when I will finally be all that Christ
saved me for and wants me to be*
(Philippians 3:12, TLB).

*G*igi, *you're never going to make it.*

Try as I would, I could never quite measure up to all I thought the Lord wanted me to be, or all *I* thought I should be. Satan, taking full advantage of my doubt, kept me in a constant state of despair. I believed him, envying those lovely, godly women with the gentle spirits, whom the Lord loves (*see* 1 Peter 3:4).

Some people just seem to have an easy time living the Christian life. Not me! And, after leaving his calling card of discouragement on the doorstep of my heart, Satan also convinced me that since I was not "perfect" I certainly had no right to minister to others. So I pulled a shell of low self-esteem about myself, cringing each time I was asked to share my faith. I felt like such a spiritual failure that it would have been hypocritical to share something I didn't believe I possessed. I remained in this state of spiritual insecurity for several years, always striving, yet continuing to fail.

One day two of my younger children, who had been playing in the yard, came running into the kitchen, their eyes bright with excitement, their little hands hidden behind their backs. Laughing with delight, they produced a large bunch of flowers they had gathered from the yard. I showed my surprise and joy with a big hug for each one, and ran to find a vase.

As I hurriedly arranged a bouquet, the flowers kept tumbling out. Then I noticed that the stems were all too short. The children had picked only the blossoms! I laughed to myself, thinking how much I had been blessed by their gift of love, however imperfect.

Suddenly a beautiful realization dawned—*We don't have to be perfect to be a blessing.* We are asked only to be real, trusting in His perfection to cover our imperfection, knowing that one day we will finally be all that Christ saved us for and wants us to be.

The Burr

Do everything without complaining or arguing
(Philippians 2:14).

They tell a story here in the South about a man and an old hound dog. When the man pulled up in front of a country store, he noticed the dog, howling on the front porch. Eying him curiously, the man went on inside. Several minutes later the dog was still howling.

When the customer was ready to pay for his purchases, he asked the old man at the cash register, "What's the matter with your dog?"

"Oh," shrugged the clerk, "he's probably just sitting on a cocklebur."

"Well," asked the visitor, "why doesn't he get off?"

The old man grinned and replied, "Guess he'd rather howl."

This old hound dog reminds me of some people I know, including myself. Some people seem to howl about everything. Just listen the next time you are standing in line at the grocery store or sitting at the beauty shop. I hear complaints about everything and everyone, from the president to movie stars. I hear a lot more complaining than I do expressions of gratitude. Howling seems to have become a way of life.

Satan loves to fill our lives with burrs, and he knows just how to place them where they will be the most irritating and the most uncomfortable—long lines at the checkout counter, a grumpy neighbor, a leaky washing machine, a gas gauge that reads "empty" when you are in a hurry.

Some burrs take the form of tedious chores and responsibilities. Others are disguised as a negative attitude or a sharp tongue. And there are even two-legged burrs— people who make demands on our time and energy when it is already depleted. Some burrs prick all-too-sensitive feelings, and others attack spiritually.

When I am bothered by burrs, I find myself doing everything except what I should do. I talk about them. I complain about them. I worry about them. I lose sleep over them. I even find that I often howl more than I pray about them.

In the Old Testament we are taught that "howling" is a sin that reaps serious consequences. An entire generation of Israelites wandered for forty years in the desert and were not allowed to enter the Promised Land because of their complaining. "And do not grumble, as some of them did—and were killed by the destroying angel" (1 Corinthians 10:10).

Scripture also tells us how to overcome the habit of howling. "Fix your thoughts on what is true and good and right. Think about things that are pure and lovely, and dwell on the fine, good things in others. Think about all you can praise God for and be glad about" (Philippians 4:8, TLB).

Not long ago I had a burr in my life that caused me much irritation, and I howled loud and long. Finally I

gave up. "Lord," I prayed, "I'm tired of this burr. But I'm even more tired of howling about it." So I began to thank Him and praise Him for what He was doing in my life through this burr. To my amazement I found that, although the burr was still there, it had lost its power to irritate.

Give Him your burrs, and He will give you the grace to overcome the habit of howling.

Am I Appetizing?

*Be careful how you behave among your unsaved
neighbors; for then, even if they are suspicious of you
and talk against you, they will end up praising God
for your good works when Christ returns*
(1 Peter 2:12, TLB).

We turned the key and opened the door. The
children could not contain their excitement
and pushed past us, racing from room to room to explore
their new home. Soon the large moving van appeared and
backed slowly up the driveway to unload our furniture.

Moving day is a scene that has been repeated many
times, for our family has lived in several foreign countries,
including France, Switzerland, and Israel, and in many
different communities in the United States.

Each time we arrive in a new location, we sense that
our neighbors don't know just what to expect. A family with
seven children is bad enough, but the fact that I am Billy
Graham's daughter and the mother of his grandchildren
brings varied reactions. Some are pleased, some are dubi-
ous, many are downright intimidated, but all are curious.

Will we quote Bible verses all day? Or preface each
sentence with "The Bible says"? Will we preach from our
back yard, or try other methods to "convert" them? Will

we condemn their lifestyle? One neighbor later admitted that he was certain God was trying to "sandwich" him when we bought the house next door! Another came to our door and found my hair in rollers.

"Oh!" he exclaimed. "*You* wear rollers?"

I guess he thought an angel arranged my hair during the night.

But they soon learn that rollers are more in vogue in our house than halos, that we mow our lawn, shop for groceries, and pay our bills like everyone else. They discover that our children argue, that I frequently scream at them to quit, that we are, in short, far from perfect—very normal, ordinary people. So they begin to relax.

But I do take my Christian witness seriously, and I am always conscious of the fact that I represent the Lord Jesus.

As a child I awoke one morning and dragged myself down the stairs to breakfast. Mother had overslept, so she had hurriedly put on her robe, then grabbed Franklin out of his crib without bothering to comb her hair or change his diaper. When I arrived in the kitchen, she was standing over the stove frying bacon, Franklin was banging on his high chair, Bunny was talking a blue streak, and Anne was silently picking at her plate. After looking around, I threw down my fork and said, "Mama, between looking at you, smelling Franklin, and listening to Bunny, I'm just not hungry!"

Now I take a critical look at our family and our lifestyle. Are we appetizing? I examine myself, my attitude toward the children, how I answer the door or the telephone, how I react when someone pushes ahead of me in line at the grocery store, how I dress, how I behave when I think no one recognizes me. Would I want *me* for a neighbor?

Do I practice my Christianity in practical ways? Do

others see Jesus in me? Do they observe patience and kindness? Am I approachable, accessible, available? When guests walk into my home, do they feel welcome? Do they feel the presence of the Lord? Are those who live around us and come in contact with us attracted to Him? Or are they "just not hungry"?

It has been said that you may well doubt the reality of your Christian experience if your life does not demand an explanation. May our lives cause others to hunger and thirst for our Lord.

But How? How? How?

could see the first rays of light as the sun made its way slowly up Little Piney Ridge. Only a few more minutes and it would burst forth, ushering in another day. Until then, I would sit at my window and savor these quiet moments.

Early morning fog still covered most of the sleepy valley below, obscuring the little town of Black Mountain that was just beginning to stir. But the tops of the Blue Ridge Mountains stood out dark and clear against the dawn. And just beneath my window, the lilac bush was heavy with dew, its large fragrant blossoms bowed with the weight, poised in anticipation of a new day. It promised to be a glorious one!

I prayed fervently, *O Lord, please let this be the day You and I get it together!*

After reading a portion of my Bible, I prayed again, giving the Lord my day. I felt so good. It was all so beautiful. Surely I wouldn't blow it today. I bounded down the stairs, inhaling the heavenly aroma of bacon and eggs emanating from the kitchen.

I tried. I really did. But my spirituality didn't even make it all the way through breakfast. First I argued with one of my sisters, then talked back to my mother when she scolded me. Then, when I realized what I had done, I became so discouraged I just gave up on that day completely.

So goes the story of my life. Trying so hard . . . and falling so short. I am a struggler. If only I could arrive at this or that spiritual plateau, or if only I could eliminate this or that problem or weakness, then I would be "worthy." Living the Christlike life just hasn't come easily for me. But the deep longing and desire to be like Him started in my childhood, continued into my teens, and followed me into marriage.

Several years later I was sitting at another window overlooking another valley. By this time I was married to Stephan and living in Switzerland. I had been reading one of the many books on victorious Christian living that now fill my shelves. And as I gazed out over the flower-strewn fields to the snow-capped Alps beyond, I suddenly found tears streaming down my cheeks. I cried out in utter frustration, "But Lord! How? How? How?"

As I sat there with my bowed head in my hands, I remembered something I had read years before: "His Father said, 'Leave that book and read the Book that thou lovest best. Thou wilt find it much simpler.' "

Perhaps I had been reading too many books, trying too hard. My heavenly Father then reminded me that I was created not to *be*, but to *belong*. For a moment I reveled in that thought. Not to be always positive, always smiling, always "up" as the books intimated—but to rest in Him and in His Word alone. It seemed too good to be true!

But it was and is true. Our part is to focus on belonging,

abiding, and He will take care of the rest. As Corrie Ten Boom used to say, "We need to quit struggling and start snuggling."

"I am the vine; you are the branches. If a man remains in me and I in him, he will bear much fruit; apart from me you can do nothing" (John 15:5).

 **P** *art Two*
Storm Watch

Who can understand how he spreads out the clouds,
how he thunders from his pavilion?
See how he scatters his lightning about him . . .
He fills his hand with lightning
and commands it to strike its mark.
His thunder announces the coming storm.
Job 36:29-30, 32-33

The Lesson of the Leaves

See how the lilies of the field grow.
They do not labor or spin
(Matthew 6:28).

Years ago, after a particularly long, hard winter, my small son and I were raking up wet leaves that had hugged the earth below the snow. We suddenly came across a patch of new, green grass under the carpet of withered brown.

"Oh!" I exclaimed. "Look! Isn't it wonderful? Isn't it beautiful? Isn't it thrilling?"

My little boy looked up at me and said, "Mama, why don't you thank God?"

I do thank Him for new life.

I recall one cold, bleak winter afternoon in Wisconsin. It was spitting snow and the wind howled around the corner of the house. Fierce gusts flung the branches of the crab apple tree against my windowpane. I was glad to be safe and warm inside.

Taking advantage of a few quiet moments, I sat curled up in a chair, drinking hot tea, my oversized sweater pulled snugly around me. As I gazed out the window, I noticed something strange. A bunch of brown, shriveled leaves clung stubbornly to the bare branches of an old oak tree. I sipped my tea and watched with curiosity as those leathery leaves held fast in the face of the surging wind.

It dawned on me how many things in my life were like those old, brown leaves.

A negative attitude.
An unforgiving spirit.
A stubborn habit.
Unyielding pride.
An ungrateful heart.

How hard I struggle to pull and pluck them off and how discouraged I become when they cling to me in spite of all my efforts.

I looked at the tree again. It wasn't struggling and striving to remove the dead leaves. *It was just waiting.* It seemed to be resting in the full and complete confidence that when spring came, the new sap would again flow through its branches . . . and the dead, ugly leaves would fall off by themselves.

I realized that this is the way it should be in my own life. I simply needed to "remain in the Vine"—the presence of Jesus Christ in His Word, as that branch remained in the oak tree. Like the branch, I needed to be available and submissive to the life-giving power of the sap—the Holy Spirit. As His life flowed through me, those old, decaying habits and ways that clung so persistently would begin to drop off all by themselves.

The snow was falling faster outside my window, the wind forming soft drifts along the edge of the yard. I continued to watch the leaves and thought, *Isn't that the way we should also deal with our children?* As a parent I feel so "responsible" that I try to pull, tear, yank, jerk, wrench,

and twist all the negative behaviors from my children.

I don't simply remind my children of something they should or should not have done; I hover over them.

I don't simply correct; I harp and lecture.

I don't just discipline my children; I often aggravate and discourage them.

We as parents often want to be so "in control" that we strive to extract all the brown leaves from their lives. As a result, we fail to allow our children to discover the voice of their own conscience.

I continued to watch the winter storm, laughing as I pictured myself climbing the oak tree to pull and twist off all those brown leaves. And yet that was exactly what I was doing with my children.

It's not that we don't discipline. Scripture instructs us to discipline, correct, guide, and direct our children. But too often we attempt to do the Holy Spirit's job for Him, and thus hinder His work in their lives.

As our children grow older, we frequently try to protect them from the storms of life, or from the natural consequences of their actions. Yet these are the very things the Lord uses to loosen the stubborn, brown leaves in their lives.

Perhaps we should spend less energy and time pulling and yanking at their faults and failures and a little more energy pointing them to the source of new life. As they grow in the Lord Jesus and the sap of the Holy Spirit begins to flow through their spiritual veins, many of these brown leaves will fall off by themselves.

A few months after that windy, winter day, on a lazy summer afternoon, I was watching the children playing in the yard. I glanced over at the old oak tree. It was magnificent. Bursting with fresh life and lush green leaves.

Let us as parents "run with patience the race that is set before us, looking unto Jesus."

Fruitful Frustration

I can hear thunder rolling in the distance. The clouds gather and the sky darkens as another afternoon thunderstorm approaches. It won't be long before the children come running back into the house. And I had hoped this was going to be a good day to get some work accomplished.

Sure enough, five-year-old Antony, eyes filled with terror and tears, just ran in to tell me that there is an alligator in our yard that is "big enough to eat me up!"

This merits some investigation. Excuse the interruption while I go out and check. . . .

Back again. And yes, there *is* a very large alligator nestled up along the edge of the lake. But now, in addition to the thunder, lightning, and alligators, Antony has another problem. He has discovered we are having meat loaf and potatoes for dinner—which he dislikes very much. This is simply too much for him. The tears fall even faster. Well, this looks like a perfect afternoon to put aside my work, and read to him my favorite children's story, Judith Viorst's classic *Alexander and the Terrible, Horrible, No Good, Very Bad Day.*

We cuddle up in the corner of the sofa and I begin Alexander's woeful account:

> I went to sleep with gum in my mouth and there is gum in my hair and when I got out of bed this morning I tripped on the skateboard and by mistake I dropped my sweater in the sink while the water was running and I could tell it was going to be a terrible, horrible, no good, very bad day.

Alexander ends his frustrating day with,

> There were lima beans for dinner and I hate limas. There was kissing on TV and I hate kissing. My bath was too hot, I got soap in my eyes, my marble went down the drain, and I had to wear my railroad-train pajamas. . . . When I went to bed Nick took the pillow he said I could keep and the Mickey Mouse night light burned out and I bit my tongue. . . . It has been a terrible, horrible, no good, very bad day.[1]

Little Antony's not the only one who can identify with Alexander! Most of us experience frustrating days.

Frustration is a mixture of negative ingredients like stress, irritation, conflict, fatigue, confusion, and anxiety. Sometimes frustration is caused by outward circumstances and pressures beyond our control. Other times, it results from tensions of our own making.

We experience frustration when we feel out of control, or when we are prevented from accomplishing our goals. For example, when a long-awaited, much deserved weekend away with our mate has to be canceled because one of the children suddenly falls ill, we become frustrated.

Some experience frustration because they are disorganized and never feel on top of any given situation. Others feel frustrated because they tend to be perfectionists. Nothing is done well enough to suit them. They hesitate to delegate and end up wearing themselves out trying to do it all. (I have often thought that is why the Lord gave me seven children; it keeps this perfectionist humble.)

Frustration can also be the result of expectations placed upon us by a society whose standards and values are very different from our own. Today's world often measures success by results or material gain. This can cause not only frustration but doubt of our self-worth if we don't "measure up."

Confrontation, conflict, and physical exhaustion are other sources of frustration. But there is hope. There is fruitful frustration.

A number of years ago, Stephan and I were in Israel. As we flew in a small plane from Galilee to Jerusalem, our guide pointed out several ponds where fish were hatched. He explained that until a few years ago, the only way to feed the fish was to scatter the food over the pond. What the fish did not eat turned into a foul-smelling sediment. The unpleasant job of cleaning these ponds was given to a certain young boy from a nearby *kibbutz*. Soon, this boy's frustration led him to the discovery of a technique that released fish food only when the fish were hungry—thereby eliminating the task of cleaning the smelly ponds. This method is now used worldwide.

Frustration can often pressure us into working on problems.

We can turn frustration into fruitfulness by admitting our frustrations, identifying their sources, deciding if they are "problems" or "facts of life," and then turning them into something positive.

Facts of life are burdens we have little or no control over. We must simply give them to our loving heavenly Father, and leave them there. Recently I went through such an experience, and it was difficult to "let go and let God" (*see* Psalm 46:10, NASB; 2 Corinthians 12:9; 2 Thessalonians 1:11). But with His help, I did, and this simple act released me from much of the anxiety I was experiencing.

Problems, on the other hand, are things we do have control over. These must be identified, worked on, and kept in their proper perspective.

There are not always easy answers for our frustrations. Some problems are not solved readily. Some have no solutions. But in my own life, I have discovered that the Lord has often allowed difficult, frustrating experiences in order to exercise and tighten my spiritual muscles. It was during these times that I learned to depend on Him and His strength, and discovered with Paul, that His grace is sufficient for me, that His strength is made perfect in my weakness (*see* 2 Corinthians 12:9).

It's a fact. Even on days when life serves you meatloaf and you have an alligator in your yard.

Note

1. Judith Viorst, *Alexander and the Terrible, Horrible, No Good, Very Bad Day* (New York: Atheneum Press, 1972).

The Sudden Storm

God is our refuge and strength,
an ever-present help in trouble
(Psalm 46:1).

y tired feet felt soothed by the soft, powdery sand. The quiet water calmed my soul as I watched it change from azure to deep blue to gray, reflecting the sky above. How I envied its stillness and depth.

I was tired. Physically, mentally, and emotionally. I had recently undergone surgery and needed some rest. It was good—so good—to be away from my responsibilities.

What luxury to awaken slowly this morning when I had finally had enough uninterrupted sleep.

How wonderful to enter a clean kitchen, pour a cup of coffee, and sit with my Bible—without first wiping away the pancake syrup or soggy Frosted Flakes.

No dogs to feed. No piles of dirty clothes. No cartoons blaring on the TV. No lunches to make. No children asking dozens of questions. No dishwasher. No vacuum cleaner. Just the gentle lap of surf against sloping sand and the chirping of birds in softly swaying palm trees.

Just peace . . . and quiet.

Later that morning, I sat in the sand watching a small crab darting sideways into the hole he was digging, only to emerge moments later with sand he either threw or spit out, I couldn't tell which. All the while his watchful eyes rotated wildly on his small head.

I marveled at the creativity of God. Surely He had a sense of humor to create such a creature.

I watched as lovers strolled hand in hand down the beach. With a touch of envy, I observed deep sea divers preparing to plunge into the mysteries below. I followed a small sailboat listing in the breeze until it rounded the bend out of sight, and admired brightly colored parasails floating through the blue sky.

The warm water tickled my toes and caressed my legs. This was serenity.

Suddenly, as if from nowhere, large drops of rain began to pelt down on me. Faster and faster. A downpour.

Quickly retreating to the safety of a covered terrace, I sat on a towel watching the rain . . . considering the sudden storm.

How like life.

Not too many months before, I was driving to a Bible study. I remember the place on I-95 when the thought hit me. *Lord, my life is going so well right now. It is smooth, gentle, regular—even predictable.* It reminded me of the gentle regular lapping of the surf I had just left.

The children were all doing well in school, Stephan was finally able to take a little time off, our marriage was a blessing in spite of our heavy responsibilities, we were all in good health, I had help in the home, and enough time

to minister to others outside of my home to make me feel useful.

I feel good right now, Lord, I prayed. *I feel fulfilled— thank You.*

A few weeks later things began to change. We had a serious financial setback and Stephan had to work longer hours. I began to have physical problems, culminating in surgery. One of our children encountered difficulties in school which ended with him running away from home.

My housekeeper of eleven years felt God leading her back up North, so my ministry outside of the home came to a standstill.

These were only a few of the storms that seemed to hit our family within a short period of time.

It seemed the sudden storm had developed into a steady downpour of problems—one after another—with little reprieve between.

How often in our lives sunshine suddenly turns to rain, repose turns to turmoil, and calm quickly becomes calamity. Just when things seem to be getting better or running smoother or becoming quieter, some storm hits that shatters the stillness.

I couldn't help asking the Lord *why.*

I was led to the first chapter of the little book of James. Here we are told to consider it "pure joy" whenever we face trials of many kinds.

I noticed the word *whenever.* James did not say *if.* Trials and storms are predictable. They're to be expected. But more than that, they are allowed for our spiritual growth. James goes on to say that it is in the storms of life that we develop patience, steadfastness, and endurance so that we are able to develop spiritually.

As I sat on the little covered porch watching the storm subside, I reflected on the fact that although the sunshine in my own life had often been shadowed by storms, it was also a fact that I had grown closer to my Lord during the times of turbulence. I had clung to Him, depended upon Him, rested in Him. And, just as this porch had offered protection from today's sudden storm, so I had found refuge in the person of Christ.

I glanced down and saw that the curious little crab had also sought refuge on the covered terrace. Now that the sun was once again peeking out from behind the clouds, he scurried off to continue his excavations.

Watching his hurried retreat, I thought, *So much like life. We endure the storm, receive strength and fortitude, and then continue on.*

I got up and went to fix some lunch.

The Defense

 was very angry. My hands shook and my voice trembled.

Why were we receiving such vicious, hurtful treatment? We had searched our hearts and before God, could find nothing that merited the treatment being unleashed against us.

I felt hurt and frustrated. We had tried to correct the situation and things just seemed to get worse. The condition continued to deteriorate although I had written, called, and done all we knew to do to show love in spite of the fact that we were being treated so harshly.

My first reaction to this latest episode of disparagement was to lash out.

I soaked in the warm water in my bathtub, preparing a speech. I decided that I had written enough sweet letters; now I was going to let go and let them have it.

I used big, impressive words, and strong, though

polite, language. It was a powerful speech, and as I prepared for bed, I felt proud of it.

Later, I took my yellow legal pad and sat down. The rush of the mountain stream outside my bedroom window was almost drowned out by the sound of katydids. What a wonderful summer evening. If only I weren't so upset, and could enjoy it!

I began to write until I had filled several pages. I looked down at my watch, and with a start realized it was getting late. Even the katydids were quiet, and all the emotion and effort it had taken to write the letter made me feel especially tired.

I decided it would be better to sleep on it. If I felt the same way in the morning, I would mail it.

I awoke feeling much the same. For some time this situation had persisted, and I was now at my wits end. I had really taken all I could take.

Brewing a cup of coffee, I sat down at the kitchen table to have my devotional time.

"Love your enemies," I read, "do good to those who hate you, bless those who curse you, pray for those who mistreat you" (Luke 6:27-28).

I couldn't believe my eyes. All those verbs.

Love
Do good
Bless
Pray for
And all concerning those who cause us harm.

What was the Lord trying to tell me?

Wanting more then anything to be in His will and to have His mind about this matter, I asked Him for His perspective. As I did, I was reminded of Paul's words to the

Romans: "Do not take revenge, my friends, but leave room for God's wrath . . . Do not be overcome by evil, but overcome evil with good" (Romans 12: 19,21).

I slowly realized that the Lord would be the one to defend us. He was saying, "Gigi, be still and know that I am God. . . . If I am for you who can be against you?"

I had to let Him defend us. In His own way. In His own time.

Finishing my coffee, I took out the legal pad and rewrote the letter.

I was still honest, telling the truth in love, but the defensiveness was gone. I would allow God to make it right—to work out all things for His glory.

I was still hurt, but the anger was gone. The Lord reminded me that He was in control of all things, and I felt the weight of this whole affair begin to slip from my shoulders. With His help, I would continue to love, do good, pray . . . and leave the results to Him.

Beyond the Storm

I t was evening as I climbed aboard the jumbo jet. I was tired. It had been a hectic, emotionally stormy week. I had endured more than the usual schedule changes, telephone calls, interruptions, children's activities, and arguments.

I settled into my seat, relieved to see that the plane was nearly empty. Maybe I could get some much-needed rest. The giant plane took off and climbed up over the condominium complexes hugging the white stretch of beach bordering the deep blue of the Atlantic Ocean. As we passed over Ft. Lauderdale, I looked down at the twinkling lights reflected in the many canals and waterways and realized why our city is referred to as the Venice of America. I never tire of the beauty of south Florida.

I settled down, grateful for the quiet. Suddenly I noticed dark, ominous clouds off the left side of the wing. Soon, bolts of lightning began to streak across the dark clouds.

I sat mesmerized by this vicious storm only a few miles away. It was frightening, yet fascinating. It brought to mind many of the tempests I had experienced in my life. Financial storms, physical storms, emotional storms, relational storms. So many different types of storms with varying degrees of intensity.

Some had been as fearful and terrifying as this large thunderhead; others had been sudden. Some storms had resembled a weather front that moves in and won't go away.

As I sat there contemplating the severity of the weather outside the window—and the storms that had raged within my own life—I suddenly saw beyond the storm.

There, along the horizon, was one of the most magnificent sunsets I had ever been privileged to witness. Brilliant gold blending with deep crimson fading into multiple shades of yellow, peach, apricot, and rose. What absolute, breathtaking beauty.

I watched with wonder and awe.

From the vantage point of forty-two thousand feet up, I knew that at any moment this formidable thunderstorm would probably hit our home west of Ft. Lauderdale. But I could also see beyond the storm, and knew that in just a short space of time, those who would be hit by the storm, would also experience incredible beauty.

I was suddenly aware of how God must look upon the storms that hit our lives.

Often I have been in the midst of a fearful squall, and like the disciples, cried out, "Lord, don't you care? Don't you see that I can't take any more?"

Of course He cares. In 1 Peter He reminds us that He

cares for us. That we are His personal concern. But, from His vantage point, He also sees the glory that is to follow.

His message? Don't be discouraged in the midst of life's storms. Be assured that God does care. That His plans for us include a future and a hope.

Beyond the storm lies incredible glory.

Hope

*There is a time for everything,
and a season for every activity under heaven:
a time to be born and a time to die*
(Ecclesiastes 3:1-2).

I whisked the children out the door for school, then quickly straightened up the house, just hitting the high points. Rushing to my room, I threw on some clothes, touched up my hair and face, and ran out to the car. The hospital was only a mile from the house but the twenty-five-mile-an-hour speed limit made it seem much longer.

I glanced out at the morning.

Crisp, clean air, fluffy white clouds scattered over a big blue sky, palm trees swaying . . . what a day to be born!

We were expecting our second grandchild any moment, and I wanted to be there when this newest member of our family arrived.

I entered the waiting room to be greeted by Lisa's parents, brother, and our small grandson.

What excitement!

What anticipation!

While we anxiously waited, I asked about Julie, Lisa's only sister.

Julie lay quietly at home. Barely able to move now, her long battle with cancer was seemingly near the end.

Miraculously free of pain, she slept most of the time. But, now and then she would awaken, searching for the face of her young husband as if to try and gain a bit of strength from the love in his eyes.

Their eyes would meet, she would smile, then quietly fall asleep again.

We had spent many hours praying for Julie's healing from this ghastly disease. But, with each labored breath, she seemed nearer being ushered into the presence of her Lord and Savior, Jesus Christ.

Suddenly the waiting room door burst open.

"It's a girl!" a beaming Stephan-Nelson announced. It was as impossible for him to conceal his pride as it was for us to conceal our excitement.

"Lisa and the baby are fine," our son continued. We all rushed to the nursery window, so grateful for her safe arrival. As we stood around waiting for that first glimpse, Stephan-Nelson said, "Her name is Hope, and she has blue eyes and golden-red hair."

A hush fell upon us as our eyes moistened over with emotion.

The name Hope had been chosen because of the hope we all held that blue-eyed, red-haired Aunt Julie would somehow be miraculously healed.

Julie, too weak to come to the hospital, would have to wait two days before holding baby Hope in her arms.

When she did, she held her close and gazed into her eyes.

"You're beautiful," she whispered.

We continued to have faith and to believe that somehow, God would touch Julie, just as He had touched Simon Peter's mother-in-law, taken her by the hand, and lifted her up. We prayed that Julie, too, would be able to get out of bed and begin to serve again.

Valentine's Day dawned bright and clear. I got dressed and decided to stop by Stephan-Nelson's office to ask if he had time to go to lunch with his mother. Although the weather was just about perfect, as I drove into town, I noticed a big storm brewing out over the Everglades. I hoped it would not ruin this special day.

Stephan-Nelson was not in, so I asked a co-worker where he was.

"Oh, Mrs. Tchividjian," the girl replied, "Julie just died."

My heart sank. I felt hot, then cold.

All of our hope for healing . . . gone. Just like that. And of all days, on Valentine's Day.

Why? How could this be?

Hadn't the birth of baby Hope only five days before been a sign of hope?

I drove home trying to allow it all to sink into my heart.

In the house, I sank into a chair. And cried. And prayed. And tried to think.

I tried to imagine all of the emotions my son's family was experiencing.

The terrible loss for the young husband.

The grief of the parents.
The heartbreak of seemingly unanswered prayer.
The questions.
The doubts.
The despair.
The deep darkness that would not disappear with the morning.

The room suddenly grew dark, and I knew the storm was now overhead. I heard a few large drops of rain hit the roof, and then the downpour. But the storm outside could not compare with the storm brewing in my heart.

Hadn't we all asked in faith believing? Hadn't God promised to answer the prayers of those who believed?

What went wrong?

Although we had prayed, "Your will be done," and in reality Julie was now eternally healed, we had asked for *earthly* healing.

I searched for answers, but couldn't find any that satisfied. The Lord doesn't always choose to give us answers or explanations. I longed for words of comfort and strength to share, but they sounded so hollow. My thoughts drifted to the refrain of a tune:

> When answers aren't enough, there is Jesus,
> He's more then just an answer to your prayer,
> When your heart would find a safe
>   and peaceful refuge
> And answers aren't enough, He's there.

I groaned with Job when he asked, "Where is now my hope," and remembered that, "My hope is built on nothing less than Jesus' blood and righteousness." I recalled Paul's words that "if only for this life we have hope in Christ, we are to be pitied more than all men" (1 Corinthians 15:19).

My thoughts drifted to another friend who lost his wife after agonized prayer for her healing. "There is a greater miracle then the miracle of healing," he had told me. "There is resurrection."

Suddenly the room brightened. The ugly black thunder clouds had passed on and the sun began to ever-so-gently worm its way around the remaining clouds.

Yes, we grieve, but not as those who have no hope. We look for that blessed hope, the return of our Lord and Savior Jesus Christ. Our hope is in our eternal life which God, who cannot lie, promised before the world began.

Until that day, we have blue-eyed, red-haired baby Hope to remind us of eternity and the comfort that one day soon, we will be watching Julie and Hope walking hand in hand in Heaven.

We continue to miss Julie.

There will always be a hole in each of our hearts shaped like Julie, freckles and all.

Things are not the same without her. Especially on Valentine's Day.

The Day the
Sandman Came

*You know that the testing of your faith develops
perseverance. Perseverance must finish its work
so that you may be mature and complete,
not lacking anything*
(James 1:3-4).

The afternoon thunderstorm had rolled on and the sun was out once again. Soon the children would crawl out from various corners of the house like so many little bugs after dark. Summer was only half over, and I had six more weeks to try to find creative ways to entertain six energetic children.

Suddenly I spotted the old sandbox.

"Let's fix it up!" I announced.

After gathering the troops, we pulled weeds and cleaned up the area. Then we were off to the local sand company. We had been told that our sandbox would require about five tons of sand. Not really knowing how much five tons would be, we took the van, loaded with buckets and old garbage cans.

With our containers filled, we returned home. Our son backed the van around, leaving a few tire tracks in the wet grass. He dumped the sand and drove back across the grass, this time breaking off a small tree limb in the process and receiving a sharp tongue-lashing from me.

When we looked at the sandbox, we saw that the sand filled only one small corner! A quick call to the company confirmed that, for a small fee, they would deliver the remaining sand that very afternoon. I cautioned them to send their lightest truck and their best driver, as the yard was wet from recent heavy rains.

When the truck arrived, I showed the driver where the sandbox was located and, as he began to back around the house, I followed. To my dismay, the truck loaded with sand was making deep trenches in the soft ground. Maneuvering the rear of the truck into position, he took several large branches from overhanging trees. Oh, well! Maybe the children's enjoyment of their sandbox would be worth all the trouble!

Then it happened. The driver got stuck in the wet earth. The more he accelerated, the deeper he sank, until his big truck began to slide down the hill toward the lake, plowing a gaping hole on its way. By now, he was in up to his axles, and I suggested we call the sand company and ask for help.

An hour later, a large tow truck arrived. The driver backed around, leaving more black trenches, and put a cable around truck number one. The more he tugged and pulled, the larger the hole grew. Then he, too, got stuck, digging into the yard, breaking sprinkler pipes, splintering branches, and uprooting small trees.Another call to the company resulted in truck number three, the cab of an eighteen-wheeler!

About eight o'clock that evening, after five-and-a-half hours of mass destruction, all three trucks pulled out of our yard. When we assessed the damage, there was the gaping hole, the broken sprinkler pipes sticking up like so

many broken bones, ugly black tracks across our lawn, ripped trees, and five tons of sand—not in, but *beside* the sandbox. And a bill for the sand and two tow trucks!

Much later, as I was tucking the eight-year-old in bed, he prayed: "And thank You, Lord, for the exciting day and for all the entertainment we had!"

In spite of everything, I had to chuckle. I hadn't thought about the day's disasters in terms of "entertainment." Nor had I thought about thanking God for all the excitement. Yet falling asleep with thanksgiving on your tongue—no matter what the circumstances—was certainly an improvement over what had been on *my* tongue and heart that evening.

No wonder the Scripture entreats us to be more like children!

The Argument

He walked out, closing the door firmly behind him. I heard the car drive away and, with a heavy, aching heart, I leaned against the closed door. Hot, angry tears filled my eyes, spilled over, and ran down my cheeks.

How had it happened? How had things built to this point? Neither of us had intended our little discussion to develop into a heated disagreement. But it was late, and we had both experienced a hard day.

Stephan had risen early to drive one of the car pools. Then he had seen several patients with difficult, heartbreaking problems. An emergency had taken up his lunch break, so he had been behind schedule for the rest of the afternoon. When he finally left the office, he hit a traffic jam on the freeway, arriving home tense and tired to a wife and seven children all demanding his attention.

I, too, had endured a difficult day after a sleepless night with the baby. Besides the normal activities involved with running a home, the rain had kept us confined indoors all day. It was hot and humid, and the children were more quarrelsome than usual, amusing themselves by picking on each other. Between settling arguments and soothing hurt feelings, I managed to get dinner on the table. But I hadn't taken the time to comb my hair or freshen my make-up, and Stephan could sense my frustration when he came in.

Finally, when the kitchen was clean, the small children bathed and tucked into bed, and the teenagers talked out, Stephan and I found ourselves alone in our bedroom, trying to discuss a minor problem. It soon blew out of proportion. Angry feelings were vented, words spoken that we did not mean, and then—the slammed door and retreating car.

I slumped into a chair, dissolving into tears of discouragement and disappointment in myself. How long was it going to take to learn my lesson? The late-night hours after a long day is not the time for arguing, but for comfort, encouragement, and loving. As I sat there, I remembered that I had been so busy trying to handle the home front, keeping everything and everyone under control, that I had not spent time with the Lord that day. I had even failed to pray for Stephan. No wonder things had not gone well for him.

I glanced in the mirror and saw red, puffy eyes, no make-up, and hair in disarray. I saw lines of fatigue and tension where there should have been tenderness and love, and I understood Stephan's desire to get away and cool off.

I fell on my knees beside the chair, asking the Lord to forgive me and to fill me with His Holy Spirit so I could be to Stephan all he had ever dreamed. I asked for His strength, His sensitivity, His wisdom so I could juggle my own schedule, the demands of my home and children, and

still have time to meet my husband's needs when he came home from the day's work. Then I added a timid P.S., asking Him to give Stephan a change of heart, too.

I felt peace and a sudden refreshing. I got up, washed my face, adding a little color to my cheeks and lips, combed my hair, lavishly sprayed perfume on myself, and climbed into bed to wait.

Before long, I heard the front door open and familiar footsteps in the brick hallway. Our bedroom door opened quietly and Stephan stood there, his tired face and kind, loving eyes drawing me like a magnet. I flew into his arms. Later, our loving erased the last traces of frustration and anger. Clinging to each other as we fell into a much-needed sleep, I couldn't help wondering why we hadn't thought of this in the first place.

> You look at me
> and see
> my flaws;
> I look at you
> and see
> flaws, too.
> Those who love,
> know love
> deserves
> a second glance;
> each failure serves
> another chance.
> Love looks to see,
> beyond the scars
> and flaws,
> the cause;
> and scars become
> an honorable badge
> of battles fought
> and won—

(or lost)
but fought!
The product,
not the cost,
is what love sought.

* * *

God help us see
beyond the now
to the before,
and note with tenderness
what lies between
—and love the more!
                    Ruth Bell Graham

But I Don't Have It All Together!

We all sat around the table drinking coffee and talking. Suddenly one of the ladies in the group turned to me and said, "Well, after all, *you* have it all together!"

Dumbfounded, I thought to myself, *Lady, if you only knew!*

With this episode fresh in my mind, it was with reluctance that I walked to the closet and took down my suitcase. On this trip I would be addressing four thousand women on the subject of "serenity." As I selected several items of clothing, I was wondering if there was any way I could get out of this commitment. I had no business speaking on a topic I knew so little about—and was experiencing so little of in my own life.

Our family had enjoyed a lovely summer vacation in the mountains of North Carolina. After a month of sleeping late, eating well, and breathing cool mountain air, I felt rested and refreshed. But the return two-day trip in the van with nine people had all but destroyed the effects of the vacation.

When we arrived home, we received an emergency telephone call informing us of my grandmother's death, so Stephan and I repacked and hurriedly returned to North Carolina. After the funeral we called the children only to discover they were under the threat of a hurricane, and we would probably not be able to fly home. Two days and several delays later, we walked in our front door to find that the storm had flooded the living room. We were just recovering from the flood damage when my mother underwent surgery, followed by serious complications. All this on top of getting the children settled in school amid the everyday hassles of managing a large household—*and I was supposed to tell four thousand ladies how to experience serenity?!*

I went into the bathroom where I could be alone and prayed, "Lord, I can't! There is just no way I can talk to those ladies when I don't know the first thing about serenity!"

Then just as clearly, though not audibly, I heard Him say: *Gigi, you're right. You haven't experienced much serenity in your life lately. But for weeks you have prayed that what you share with those ladies would not be your message, but Mine— and I have everything to share.*

Humbly I said, "Thank You, Lord." Then I continued to pack. My burden was lifted as I submitted to Him.

It is His message—not mine.
It is His will—not mine.
It is His life—not mine.

And that day, during my address to four thousand ladies, it was His serenity—not mine!

The Vase

While dressing for dinner, I could hear the screaming and arguing all the way to my bedroom. It sounded serious, so I ran to investigate. (I find being a "policewoman" the most distasteful part of motherhood.)

I arrived just in time to see one son throw a flower vase at another. The vase flew past his head and exploded on the brick terrace. A hush fell as they looked up and found me standing in the doorway, staring at the fragments of broken pottery. After a scolding in which I expressed my disappointment at their behavior and my regret over the shattered vase, I returned to my room, leaving them silent and subdued.

Later as I passed the terrace, I saw the two culprits, their heads bent together over what had once been the vase. With a large pot of glue on the floor beside them, the two little fellows were patiently trying to piece it back together. They had made a mistake, but they were sorry and were doing their best to repair the damage.

I stood there for a moment thinking of all the times that I, too, have caused damage. How often, because of lack of self-control, have I hurled harsh words and broken a heart or fractured a relationship? How often has my insensitivity shattered someone's self-esteem? How often have I crushed a child's will or smashed his pride? How often have I damaged self-confidence and caused discouragement by harping on faults instead of praising a job well done?

Observing my children that day, I learned an invaluable lesson. Yes, we do make mistakes, but God is in the restoring business. And whatever the mistake—whether large or small, seemingly insignificant or fraught with serious consequences—we can humbly acknowledge our faults, repent, and do everything possible to repair the damage, trusting Him to mend what we cannot mend.

Never let the sense of the irreparable cause you to despair. Give your mistakes to the Lord and allow Him to "make all things new."

P.S. The boys succeeded in "repairing" the vase. That cracked, crooked, glue-covered vase is among my most treasured possessions.

The Plaques

The children had all left for school. With a busy day of writing planned, I wanted to get an early start, so I hurried to clean up the breakfast dishes. I could hear the whir of the washing machine as it spun the first load of wash. If I rushed, it would take only a few minutes to straighten the bedrooms. (The cleaning would have to wait for another day.)

I was looking forward to a few hours of productive quiet. I don't work well under pressure, but I don't work at all without it, and I had only a few days left to meet a deadline.

When the phone rang I tried to ignore it. But when it persisted, I picked up the receiver and a cheery voice on the other end asked, "Did I catch you at a bad time?"

Politely I lied: "No, it's fine." I didn't have the heart to refuse a friend who needed some encouragement.

When I finally hung up, I went to put in the second

load of wash before heading to my desk. I glanced at my watch and realized I had only an hour before my kindergartner would be home. I sat down at the desk, prayed, and began to work.

The doorbell rang.

Oh, no! I had completely forgotten it was the second Thursday of the month—the day the bug man comes.

Just as he drove away, Jerushah walked in the door. As I fixed her a peanut butter and jelly sandwich, I looked at the calendar. The next day twenty-four fifth-graders would be coming for a swimming party . . . and then I was expecting twenty for a potluck dinner that same evening.

Another week had flown past and I felt as if I hadn't accomplished anything. Panic began to rise. How would I ever finish?

I sank into a chair and buried my face in my hands, exhausted. Too much pressure and tension, complicated by six months of pregnancy, had drained me physically and emotionally. I felt completely frustrated. I wanted to meet the deadline, and yet my daily duties and responsibilities seemed to crowd in. I was tired of all the interruptions and the steady stream of small, insignificant obligations that occupied so much of my time and robbed me of the energy to accomplish what I thought were important goals.

My mind focused on the large wooden plaque which hangs above my mother's kitchen sink:

Divine Services Conducted Here Daily

Were all these routine, mundane duties really "divine services"? Was it possible that encouraging a friend, sharing my pool, picking up toys, cleaning and cooking for company, even making peanut butter and jelly sandwiches were of more eternal value than meeting deadlines?

Had I convinced myself that I was accepting these "important" speaking and writing assignments for the Lord, when in reality they were for me and my own ego? Had the temporal once again obscured the eternal? Had I allowed my priorities to become misplaced?

I opened my eyes, and they fell on another plaque, framed in bright yellow and hanging on my own wall:

Praise and Pray and Peg Away

I had to smile. I knew the Lord was using this method to speak directly to me. His direction and desire for us is not as complicated as we tend to make it. So I again bowed my head and turned over to Him my time and energy, my calendar and my schedule, asking for His wisdom and strength in coordinating the details and accepting even the interruptions as from Him. Then I got up, thanking Him and praising Him and proceeding to peg away at the next duty.

As I cleaned the remnants of the peanut butter and jelly sandwich from the table (and the floor) and wiped sticky fingers (and a stickier face), the telephone rang again.

Smiling to myself, I went willingly to answer it. I was, after all, performing a divine service.

P.S. I met the deadline, too!

"My Heart
Is Too Small"

I shall run the way of Thy commandments,
for Thou wilt enlarge my heart
(Psalm 119:32, NASB).

I t was early morning and I had a busy schedule planned. Suddenly I heard a knock at the front door. When I opened it, I groaned inwardly. There stood a friend with a tendency to create problems for herself, and she needed a sounding board. I sighed and invited her to come in.

Some time later, as we sat by the open fire, drinking coffee and watching the snowflakes swirl outside the window, she poured out her heart. I was stunned, unable to believe what I was hearing. This woman whom I had housed, fed, and helped on numerous occasions was reciting a litany of complaints and resentments toward me that wounded and confused me. By the time she left, I was bewildered and deeply hurt.

I stumbled through the rest of my day, automatically preparing dinner, carrying on conversations, and putting the children to bed. I couldn't sleep that night and lay in bed, allowing the disappointment and wounded feelings to fester into bitterness. What had given her the right to speak to me as she had—to expect so much from me? It seemed that the more I gave, the more she expected and the less she appreciated. Why was she so defensive, so thoughtless?

In the following days my offended feelings grew into what could only be called anger, but I called it "righteous indignation." Since it was painful to be around my friend, I tried to avoid her, gradually building a protective wall about myself. The weeks lengthened into months and I was still far from attempting to understand or remedy the situation. The more I thought about her unjust accusations, the more resentful I felt.

But the Lord has marvelous ways of gently rebuking us when we are not walking worthy of Him. It wasn't long before He made me aware that my attitude was anything but Christlike.

One of my younger children was acting especially cantankerous one day. He was disobedient, sassy, rude, obstinate—you name it. He blamed everyone in the family for making his life miserable. Finally, hoping to get to the bottom of things, we sat him down and asked him why his attitude was so awful.

"Well," he replied, "I guess it's because my heart is too small."

His answer struck me. *Could this be my problem, too?* Was my heart so narrow, so limited, so self-centered that I had failed to explore the reasons behind my friend's actions? Had I allowed my injured ego to close the door to the very part of me the Lord wanted to use in this woman's life? Was I suffering from a shriveled heart?

To my shame I thought of the times the Lord had graciously looked beyond my faults, which often camouflaged my own hidden needs. Instead of condemning me

along with my failures, He had gone right to the point of the need and touched it with His healing love. God is love and love is kind, not touchy; it does not hold grudges, and hardly notices when others do it wrong (*see* 1 Corinthians 13, TLB). Love always takes a second look!

Suddenly I knew the Lord expected me to deal with my friend as He always deals with me—gently, lovingly, fully forgiving. So I began to look beyond her irritating flaws and hurtful words and discovered insecurity, low self-esteem, envy, loneliness, and other difficulties she was bravely trying to cope with.

I asked the Lord to forgive my attitude and to give me compassion, wisdom, understanding, and largeness of heart (1 Kings 4:29) so that I could begin to share not only *her* burdens (Galatians 6:2), but those of the many others whose paths cross mine.

Only He has the cure for a shrinking heart.

The Battlefield

I awoke early to the soft patter of raindrops. The first rays of light were just beginning to dance behind the curtains when Stephan brought me a welcomed cup of coffee. I took my Bible from the bedside table and began a few quiet moments with the Lord.

Suddenly fighting erupted down the hall. *Why do kids argue and fight so much?* I wondered.

My quiet time was abruptly suspended as seven-year-old Antony burst into my room to file a loud complaint against his sister, Jerushah, and brother, Aram.

"Jerushah pushed me and won't let me into the bathroom—and Aram won't let me use the brush or share his gel!"

I sighed, thinking back over twenty-seven years of mothering. So many battles. So many quarrels.

Smiling in spite of myself, I remembered one particularly difficult day. Three-year-old Jerushah had been in a disagreeable mood all day. She whined, whimpered, wept, and drove us all to the ragged limits of our patience.

I tried everything. Cuddling, distractions, chiding, sending her to her room, even ignoring her. Nothing seemed to work. After dinner I instructed her to help six-year old Aram pick up their toys. She continued to be contrary and cranky. I could tell that Aram was becoming increasingly frustrated.

Finally in total exasperation he said, "Mama, do you know what I'm going to do with her?"

Expecting the worst, I answered, "No, honey. What?"

"I am going to hang a 'For Sale' sign around her neck," he replied seriously. I had to laugh, because I was tempted to do the same.

Erma Bombeck speaks for many parents when she says she remembers *how* she got the kids, but doesn't remember *why*. I am sure there are times—especially when it has rained for days and you've been cooped up in the house with feisty kids—that you, too, have wanted to sell your children. If you could find a buyer!

After years of observation, I have concluded that arguing, scrapping, tension, and even a certain amount of yelling is common and normal in the majority of active households.

Most children are going to battle. It's human nature. Our precious little babies were born in sin, and so whether we like it or not, they will soon begin to exhibit selfishness, greed, disrespect, and jealousy. There will be tensions and tears in the best of homes. There will be spats, disputes, and disagreements that at times will escalate into full-blown battles. And there will also be tired, frustrated parents reacting to all of this.

Following are a few things I've found helpful in dealing with family feuds.

Try not to overreact.

As much as I hate to admit it, I tend to be a screamer. So the children love to say or do things just to see my reaction. I have tried to learn to keep my reaction appropriate to the action. Not to give too much attention to every infraction. At times, being a good parent is knowing when to *ignore* misbehavior.

Whenever possible, allow your children to settle their own disputes.

As a young mother, I expended a huge amount of energy trying to solve every squabble. I fretted that my children didn't love one another and wondered why they couldn't get along. But as the years passed and more children arrived, I finally learned that I couldn't involve myself in every row and argument. There simply wasn't enough emotional energy to go around. Also, if I continued to police each incident, the children would never learn how to solve their own problems. So I began to allow them to sort through their own disagreements, stepping in only when "all else failed." Now, I am amazed how much better they are dealing with their disagreements.

Teach your children to accept responsibility for their own actions.

It is human nature to place blame on someone else. (Remember Adam and Eve?) But as our children grow from toddlers to teens, we must teach them to be responsible for their own actions and attitudes; to acknowledge and accept responsibility for their part in a conflict. They must also learn early to simply say "I'm sorry" when they are wrong, and to forgive when they are wronged.

We moms and dads set the example.

How do our children see us handle arguments and disagreements? Do we raise our voices in anger, or

remember that "a soft answer turns away anger"? Do they see unrelenting stubbornness or sweet reasonableness? Do they observe jealousy, greed, disrespect, and selfishness in us? Or do they witness us being "kind to one another, tenderhearted, forgiving one another"?

If children can learn how to cope with controversy, deal with disputes, and perfect the art of constructive argument from loving parents who exemplify it in their own lives, then they will be truly blessed. They will be better equipped to confront their world.

And one last word.

Don't become overly discouraged if you have problems with your children. God understands.

He has problems with His kids, too.

The Gentle Touch

I called the children in for a conference.

The past few months had been dreadfully hectic. The travel had been disruptive enough. But when you added the holidays, publishing deadlines, the wedding of our third child, and preparations to send another one away to school, it began to add up to a major household breakdown. The result was the normal lapse that children fall into when mom or dad fail to follow through. I needed more cooperation from them in performing their normal chores and responsibilities, so a confrontation was in order.

We sat in the family room.

I informed them of some serious slippage. I reminded them that they needed to faithfully do their chores and do them well if they were to continue receiving financial compensation. Together we outlined the conditions and details of the jobs. Some jobs were to be done simply because they shared our home, others they would be paid for doing. I did my best to simplify and clarify their individual responsibilities around the house and yard.

I tried not to make a big deal out of this conference as is often my tendency. I made my point and then sent them off, hoping most of the conversation would be remembered and the necessary corrections would be made.

The following morning, as I was straightening the children's rooms, I noticed that a pillow had fallen behind our fifteen-year-old's bed. I pulled out his bed to retrieve it and to my consternation, discovered candy wrappers, old sports pages, crumpled Frito bags, and cotton balls all intertwined with odds and ends of wires, speakers, tennis shoes, and shirts. Enough to fill a large grocery bag.

I was angry. Not only had I just cleaned under this bed a few weeks prior, but after the conference where I had stressed more help with their rooms, I had expected at least a semblance of an attempt to cooperate.

I contemplated dumping what I had collected all over his floor, but since the cleaning lady was supposed to vacuum, I piled all the stuff in one bag and left it. Boy, would I give it to Aram when he got home.

I hurriedly got dressed and rushed out to the car in order to keep an appointment. The radio was tuned to one of our local Christian stations. As I turned the key, the announcer was mid-sentence, describing a program that would discuss parental reprimands. Which was most effective, he asked, a tough, condemning method, or the gentle touch?

He had my attention. As I backed out of the driveway, the speaker posed a question: "If *you* had to be corrected or reprimanded for something," he said, "would you prefer screaming, harsh words, and condemnation, or a firm but gentle approach?"

128

I couldn't help but apply his words to my case against Aram. Yes, I was angry about the mess under his bed, and I had a right to be. My usual way of dealing with such things was to blast the offender, or to smother him with guilt. But, if I were to be really honest, in looking back over more then twenty-seven years of parenting, the "tirade" approach never has had a lasting effect. (Although there have been times when screaming seems the only way to get the attention of seven noisy children.) The tough, loud, condemning method, usually caused the children to become defensive, answer back, or simply tune me out so that I had to scream even louder the next time.

I thought about the times in my life when I had to be corrected. Those who screamed at me and condemned me for my mistakes only caused me to become defensive and discouraged. I never had the desire to do better after this approach, but often felt anger and resentment instead.

I considered how differently the Lord deals with me. Yes, He corrects me and reprimands me. He sometimes chides and scolds. Often He has to rebuke or reprove. But I have never had the Lord scream at me. I have never experienced harshness or been humiliated. I have never become discouraged by His discipline or angry because of His admonishments.

Suddenly I realized that the Lord had admonished me through the words of this radio preacher. Praying as I weaved through traffic, I said, "Thank You Lord, for Your gentle reproof. Thank You for once again reminding me to deal with my children as You deal with me."

Aram was in the kitchen reading the sports page when I arrived home that afternoon. I smiled at him and gave him a love pat as I passed by.

"How was your day?" I asked sweetly.

"Okay," he replied. After I made sure he found a

snack, and had finished reading the basketball statistics, I mentioned that there was a bag for him in his room.

"What is it?" he asked curiously.

"Oh, . . . you'll see."

Something in my voice or my expression—or maybe even his own conscience—aroused his suspicions. With a twinkle in his eyes and a sly smile, he asked, "You went under my bed didn't you?"

"Yes," I replied gently. "It was really a mess, and I want you to go and look in the bag at all the junk that was underneath. I don't want it to happen again. Okay?"

"Okay, Mom," he replied meekly.

The end results are not in yet, and although I expect a few candy wrappers from time to time, I do feel there will be an improvement.

More importantly, because this small incident was handled His way, there was peace, joy, and laughter in our home that evening.

The Never-Failing Source

emorized scripture can comfort and strengthen. Two of our friends were on the other side of the world when they received word that their oldest son, his wife, and their infant grandchild had all been killed in an automobile accident. Later, those friends said that it was the Scripture they had put to memory that kept them from going crazy those first few weeks.

One day we may not have the written Word, but it will be a lot more difficult to take away what we have hidden in our hearts and minds. I teach my children verses from the time they begin to talk, and it always amazes me how quickly their little minds grasp the words.

I personally find memorizing difficult . . . yet it is a simple way of abiding in the Word all during the day, no matter how busy. Just place a much-loved Bible verse or passage in the kitchen, on the ironing board, or in your jacket pocket and take it out while waiting at the doctor's office or elsewhere. I even place a verse in the car and repeat it while driving or waiting in traffic.

When Daddy's mother was in her late eighties, I went to visit her in the hospital. A short time before my visit, her doctor had come into the room and described her condition to her—which was very serious. After he had spoken, she was so upset she couldn't even speak. When the doctor was momentarily called out of the room, my grandmother instinctively turned to her Lord, whom she had known for so many years, for comfort and strength. A Bible verse she had put to memory many years before came to her mind and gave her the needed courage and assurance for her stay in the hospital.

The Word of God is a living Word; it is the person of Jesus Christ Himself revealed to us. Psalm 119 says that the Word cleanses, strengthens, delights, teaches, saves, comforts, directs, and gives understanding. What a resource!

I am so grateful that I was taught early to use this resource. To draw strength from it, to use it in seeking direction and guidance, to employ it in times of discouragement, disappointment, and loneliness.

My mother was sent away to high school in North Korea at the age of thirteen. She suffered terribly from homesickness. While alone in Korea, all she had learned was put to the test. It was there that the Living Word became a daily resource from which she could draw.

At the age of twelve, I too left home to go away to school. I can remember so well that awful gnawing feeling in the pit of my stomach that comes from being lonely and homesick. But because I had been taught early to turn to the Lord and to His Word for strength and comfort, I now look back on those days as a spiritual experience for which I will be forever grateful. I learned many things during those weeks and months about the vast resource I had in

my personal relationship with the Lord Jesus and in His Word. Since those days as a very young girl there have been many disappointments, heartaches, times of decision, times of discouragement; and each time I have gone to His Word. He has never once failed me.

For whatever life holds for you and your family in the coming days, weave the unfailing fabric of God's Word through your heart and mind.

It will hold strong, even if the rest of life unravels.

One of Those Days

The mother in a popular television program stood in the kitchen surrounded by the chaos left over from a breakfast wolfed down by children late for school. Dirty dishes were piled high beside the plugged sink; her husband had forgotten to unplug it before he left for work. As this mother surveyed the damage, she said, "No wonder some species eat their young."

I chuckled, but there really are days when we parents feel we cannot cope . . . and wonder if it is worth it all. Some years back I wrote a book entitled, *Thank You, Lord, for My Home*.

One day, while my mother was visiting, we experienced "one of those days." Mother sat observing it all from the sofa in our family room. The children were bouncing off the walls and arguing constantly over small, silly things. Suddenly I noticed that the septic tank had overflowed, so I called the plumber. Just then the doorbell rang, setting the dogs off in a chorus of barking. I opened the door only to discover the wallpaper man was standing there, ready to hang wallpaper. I had completely forgotten about him.

While I was trying to deal with the kids, start lunch, plan dinner, and get the laundry under control, the telephone rang again. Mother took out her notebook and began to write down all the activities going on that morning in the Tchividjian household.

Later, when I had a "free moment," I went into the family room, where by now Mother had written several pages. She looked up and said with a smile, "Honey, I think you should write a new book and title it, *Lord, I Thanked You Too Soon for My Home.*"

Approximately one out of every two homes eventually breaks up. Husbands no longer want the responsibility. Wives seeking significance in their lives look elsewhere for fulfillment. And children look for freedom and independence almost before they are old enough to speak.

Is it worth all the strain and stress? Has raising a family become more of a burden than a blessing? Why bother?

When I experience a difficult day and ask myself these questions, I often allow my mind to drift back to the mountains of North Carolina. I think back on some of the strong direction I received from *my* childhood home.

My home provided for my physical, emotional, and material needs. But it also provided for my deeper spiritual needs. My mother and father not only helped us with the *what* and the *how* questions of life, but also with the *why*. We had our heartbreaks and difficult passages as a family, but we never doubted our reason for living. That alone was a priceless heritage.

My home also provided security. I once asked one of my smaller children what he thought a home was and he replied, "It's a place where you come in out of the rain." The home should be a warm sanctuary from the storms of life for each

member of the family. A haven of love and acceptance. Not only children, but husbands and wives need this security.

My home provided models of love and commitment. I saw my parents "being kind one to another, tenderhearted, forgiving one another." That doesn't mean they didn't disagree at times. Mother says that if two people agree on everything, one of them is unnecessary.

My home also provided direction and discipline. We received tough love, seldom cheap sympathy. In my parents I saw examples of disciplined, yet fun-loving Christians who enjoyed their faith.

I am aware that not all of you reading this share this sort of family heritage. But there is nothing preventing you from *beginning* such a heritage for your children and grandchildren. Start by making sure of your own relationship with the Lord Jesus, and pass it on.

The home is an institution created by God. It was created for our good and for His glory. Proverbs 24:3 says, "By wisdom a house is built." I have found that the wisdom it takes to build a strong home can only come from God. "The wisdom that comes from heaven is first of all pure and full of quiet gentleness. Then it is peace-loving and courteous. It allows discussion and is willing to yield to others; it is full of mercy and good deeds. It is wholehearted and straightforward and sincere" (James 3:17, TLB).

What a beautiful picture of a Christian home! But it takes more than what I or my husband can put together to achieve this kind of atmosphere. Parenthood brims with incomparable privileges as well as sober responsibilities, and we don't always have the wisdom or strength or patience to deal with them. But at any time we can call on the One who does.

We don't have to be "perfect" or have "perfect families," but we do have to be real . . . and allow the reality of the Lord to shine through.

Unchecked Emotion

 looked into the eyes of my friend sitting across the table.

Eyes filled with hurt and brimming with ready tears.

The soft pink table cloth reflected the light of the single candle. It cast a warm glow over her beautiful yet troubled face. She was stretched just about as far as she could be without snapping, and I was worried.

I asked questions. I tried to encourage, but primarily I just let her talk.

Her heavy heart poured out one hurt after another, one frustration on top of another.

So much gossip.
So many whisperings and misquotes.
So much misunderstanding.
So many misconceptions and false assumptions.
So little real communication.
So little love and understanding.

So few questions asked, so many "knowing statements" proclaimed.

So little trust and respect.

Broken confidences.

Severed friendships.

Rumor mills.

I longed to be of comfort; to help my friend carry this load. Hers was a difficult situation. Like so many that we face in life, this one had no right and wrong. Both sides had valid arguments, good points, rational reasons, and real issues. But, unchecked emotion had turned rational, reasonable men and women into unreasonable reactionaries. Unchecked emotion had turned a viable, workable problem into a hurtful, divisive situation that was quickly becoming irreversible.

Emotion. One of God's most beautiful gifts. What would life be without emotion?

Love, joy, tears, passion, tenderness.

Feeling and expressing emotion is one of the great pleasures of life. Yet how often Satan chooses to use this gift for his own evil and destructive purposes. No wonder one of the things we know God hates is sowing discord.

How many marriages have been destroyed because of uncontrolled passion, or an overly sensitive, susceptible nature?

How many children hurt because of harsh words and volatile reactions by irrational parents?

How many friendships broken because of an indiscriminate emotional outburst?

Ungoverned emotion usually clouds the real issues. It fogs the mind and frustrates the heart. It coddles fickle, erratic feelings that cause inconsistent thoughts and actions instead of the calm, clear, convictions required to solve most problems.

James puts it this way, "For where envying and strife are, there is confusion. . . ." Wherever there are relationships of any kind, whether in a marriage, family, church, friendship, or office, there will be challenges and difficulties. There will be obstacles to overcome and problems to solve. But, unchecked emotion will only intensify the problem. Whether it be heated words and actions, or calculated cool contempt, both will cause untold harm and irreversible damage if not placed under the lordship of Christ.

Many of the situations we face require much wisdom and understanding, and only the wisdom of God can help solve many of our problems. James tells us that this wisdom is first of all pure and full of quiet gentleness. Then it is peace-loving and courteous. It allows discussion and is willing to yield to others; it is full of mercy and good deeds. It is wholehearted, straightforward, and sincere.

I continued to listen to my friend. At this point, it was all that I could do. But, as we said goodbye, I walked away with this prayer on my lips:

> May the mind of Christ my Savior
> Live in me from day to day
> By His love and power controlling
> All I do and say.[1]

Note
_____

1. Bruce Greer, *May the Mind of Christ My Savior*, ©1986, Word Music.

Failure Isn't Final

The Lord will fulfill his purpose for me;
your love, O Lord, endures forever
(Psalm 138:8).

This time I had really blown it.

It was one of those days you wish could be rewound—and then erased!

Since we had experienced flood damage, the carpet men had been at the house all day, replacing water-stained carpet. With everything removed from the rooms, I had decided to do some thorough cleaning. As usual, I overextended myself. By supper time I was totally exhausted. McDonald's would just have to do the cooking! So when everyone was ready, we piled into the car.

On the way, Stephan had to stop at the bank. I double-parked the car while he ran in. Glancing in my rear view mirror, I saw a large, older-model car, driven by an elderly lady with flaming red hair and a face that matched. She was becoming increasingly agitated. I was just about to move the car up when she blasted her horn.

I don't know what possessed me, but after my whirlwind

day, this was the last straw! I decided not to move. She gave another long, loud blast which just reinforced my stubborn refusal to budge, and I motioned her to pass me. As angry as she was, she managed to maneuver the big car around and pulled up beside me.

Then she lowered her window and began to yell.

I blew her a kiss.

That did it! She went crazy. She screamed, stuck out her tongue, then stormed out of her car at me, yelling, threatening me, calling me names. Heads began to turn. Passersby stopped to watch. I locked the door and wanted to crawl in a hole.

About this time Stephan came out of the bank, wondering what in the world all the commotion was about. The red-headed grandmother returned to her car, muttering and shaking her head. We continued on to McDonald's, but I was too distraught to eat.

Amy Carmichael once said, "The best thing for our ease-loving souls is to be made thoroughly ashamed of ourselves." I was ashamed, all right! So ashamed that for several nights I had a hard time sleeping. Although I hadn't lost my temper, I had been stubborn and selfish, insensitive and un-Christlike. And I couldn't apologize! I prayed for the little lady with the flaming hair. I was sorry I had allowed my human nature to drown out the quiet, gentle voice of the Holy Spirit who was prodding me to demonstrate the love of Christ.

Jesus would have simply moved the car. I had failed Him once again.

But as Jill Briscoe has said, "It is hard to remember when you're down physically and have blown it spiritually, when you're wiped out emotionally and feel ostracized socially—that *failure isn't final!*"

I was grateful for a Lord who knows how frail we are, who stands ready to forgive our failures. He doesn't want us to become discouraged or paralyzed by them, but to confess them, accept His forgiveness, and learn from them.

And if you're the little red-haired lady I offended in the parking lot, please forgive me!

Next time, by God's grace, I'll move the car.

With a smile.

Maybe.

The Revelation

A shiver ran through me.

I wasn't dressed warmly enough for the damp, night air.

I sat huddled on the little wooden bench down by the lake.

It was an especially dark night, with no moon to reflect upon the still water. Only a few stars flickered between the clouds.

Shivering again, I tucked my legs up under me. I wasn't sure if the chill was from the cold air or from the despair in my heart.

My problem seemed so much bigger than I was. Our dearly-loved teenage son had run away from home. My cheeks were streaked with tears. I had no concept of how long I had been sitting there, crying out to the Lord.

Please reveal Yourself to me. I need to feel You near. I need evidence of Your presence.

The pine trees rustled gently overhead, moved by an unseen breeze.

How I longed for a visible sign, a rustling of His presence, a soft breeze of the Holy Spirit.

Please Lord, just a special little light up in the dark pines. Then I will know that You are here and that You care.

Darkness prevailed. The lake lapped quietly against a piece of coral rock.

I felt someone approach. Lovingly, Stephan, placed a jacket around my shoulders and then quietly slipped away.

Soon, one by one, the house lights went out, and the darkness intensified. I was surrounded by quiet dark. I felt so alone.

Finally, cold and discouraged, I uncurled myself from the bench, and giving a last longing look over my shoulders up into the pines, I climbed the hill and crawled into bed.

Morning arrived all too soon. I was emotionally exhausted. I stumbled into the kitchen going through the motions of fixing breakfast and getting the children off to school.

With a heavy heart I began to straighten the house, once again asking the Lord to reveal Himself.

I was beginning to make the bed, when the phone rang. "Gigi," I heard the familiar voice of a friend say, "I just wanted you to know that I love you and am praying for you."

A few minutes later, the phone rang again. "Gigi, I just wanted you to know that you have been on my mind lately. Are you all right?" She assured me of her love and prayers.

All during the day, in phone call after phone call, loving friends offered love, concern, and support.

That evening, two friends called to say they were coming over to pray with us.

Suddenly, I realized the Lord *had* revealed Himself to me . . . again and again . . . all day long . . . lovingly and tenderly.

I was looking for a light in my darkness and He sent more then one. I asked Him to reveal Himself and His love to me in a special way. And He did. Not through night whispers, mysterious rustlings, or glimmers in the tree-tops, but in a way that I could feel. Through His people.

Humbly I bowed my head. *Thank You, Lord.*

"Carry each other's burdens, and in this way you will fulfill the law of Christ" (Galatians 6:2).

Part Three
Clear Skies

Trust in the Lord and do good;
dwell in the land and enjoy safe pasture.
Delight yourself in the Lord
and he will give you
the desires of your heart.

Commit your way to the Lord;
trust in him and he will do this:
He will make your righteousness shine
like the dawn,
The justice of your cause like the noonday sun.

Psalm 37:3-6

The Tree

I clutched my shawl around me. The night air in Jerusalem can be chilly, especially in December.

Standing on the balcony of our apartment, I watched the stars twinkling against the ebony sky and couldn't help wondering if the sky looked something like this on the night Jesus was born. I glanced in the direction of Bethlehem, which lay only a few miles away. Somehow, it just didn't seem much like Christmas.

No bright lights dangling from street corners. No Christmas carols blaring from the radio. No Santas in red suits. No Salvation Army bell ringers. Except for the bus-loads of tourists stopping to view the traditional nativity site, there was scant evidence of the celebration of the birth of Christ.

I surveyed the hills around me. In each window of the apartment buildings dotting the landscape, Hanukkah candles gave off a soft glow. Happy sounds of Israeli families celebrating the Festival of Lights drifted across the valley, a painful reminder of how much I missed my own family, thousands of miles away. Soon, they would be gathering around the open fireplace, singing carols, and exchanging the gaily wrapped gifts placed under the Christmas tree.

I thought of our apartment where Stephan and I lived, bare and devoid of all but a few signs that Christmas was only days away. Here in Israel, it wasn't possible to purchase a Christmas tree. Nor could we go into the surrounding hills and cut one down that had been so lovingly planted by Jews from around the world in the successful land reclamation program.

I sighed and turned to go in. Glancing once more at the heavens, I breathed a quick prayer.

Lord . . . please make this holy season in this ancient place—this place You visited so long ago—something special this year.

The next day as we left our apartment to do some errands, our Jewish neighbors came running across the parking lot to meet us.

"Would you like a Christmas tree?" they asked.

A Christmas tree? I had trouble believing my ears.

We assured them we would love to have a tree, but didn't know of anyplace to buy one.

"Oh, you don't have to buy it," they answered. "We've heard that on December 22, in the center of town, trees will be given away. Knowing that you are Christians, we thought you might like to have one."

We warmly thanked our neighbors, and on the designated day we went to see about this strange phenomenon . . . a Christmas tree lot in Israel!

Somehow, it was true. We selected a lovely evergreen

154

and placed it in the trunk, hoping no one would think we had cut it down. As we unloaded it at our apartment we noticed the tag attached to the tree: "Compliments of the Jewish Tourist Agency."

Collecting ornaments was like a scavenger hunt. We found a string of lights in a dusty corner of a department store; a few bright balls in another. We popped popcorn and lit candles. And it was beginning to look a lot like Christmas.

As I hung the ornaments and strung the popcorn, I reflected on the spiritual heritage this little country had given me. As much as I longed to see my family, as much as I missed the familiar mountains of home, my true roots were not so much in the soil of North Carolina as here . . . in Israel . . . in Bethlehem.

Since a small child I had been acquainted with the geography and history of this land. I smiled to myself, suddenly realizing I knew more names of ancient cities and towns here in Israel than I did in North Carolina.

I climbed up on a chair to rearrange an errant string of popcorn. I thought, *If only those who live in this land could know that Messiah, the Son of David, has already come. If only they could realize that Jesus was either a liar, an ego maniac making wild and crazy claims, or that He is who He claimed to be . . . the very Son of God.*

I climbed down and stepped back to examine my work. As I stood there admiring our little tree, I suddenly realized just how significant the tree is in the Christmas story. It reminds us not only of Bethlehem, but also of Calvary.

"For God so loved the world that He gave His only Son. . . ."

Jesus was born for the expressed purpose of going

155

from the cradle to the cross. For me. For us all.

My prayer had been answered. The tree had focused my attention on the significant, causing this Christmas to be very special. Yes, we had less. Less gifts. Less decorations. Less family. Less distractions.

But we also had more. More love and appreciation. More time and perspective to weigh the true meaning of Christmas. More to cherish and adore. More of Him.

> There will be less someday—
>   much less,
>   and there will be More;
>   less to distract
>   and amuse;
>   More to adore
>   less to burden and confuse
>   More, to undo
>   the cluttering of centuries,
>   that we might view
>   again, That which star
>   and angels
>   pointed to;
>   we shall be poorer—
>   and richer;
>   stripped—and free:
>   for always there will be a Gift
>   always a Tree.
>   Ruth Bell Graham

"Mothers Together"

My heart flooded with pride as I took my seat next to Stephan. I placed child number seven (not quite five years old) on the other side of me, close enough to grab or pinch, whichever became necessary first. I glanced down the pew and chuckled to see that Stephan, myself, and our children filled up the entire second row. All seven were dressed in their Sunday best. The boys looked so handsome and the two girls especially lovely on this day.

Following the call to worship, our pastor asked the men to come forward and kneel at the altar, dedicating themselves and the worship service to the Lord. I thought my heart would burst with gratitude as my five sons knelt beside their father. How blessed I was on this Mother's Day!

My thoughts drifted to what seemed like just a few short years ago. I was seventeen and a new bride living in Switzerland. A month after my wedding, when I discovered I was not "with child," I burst into tears thinking I would never have children. I am sure the Lord must have smiled, but He granted me "the desires of my heart," and ten months later our first son was born. I remembered the joy I felt as I celebrated that first Mother's Day as a mother.

My thoughts continued, recalling another Mother's Day a couple of years later.

I awoke that Sunday morning to the sound of bells. The valley was alive with them. The tinkling cow bells with the tolling church bells.

Opening the heavy wooden shutters covering the windows in our small chalet, I gazed in wonder at the beauty before me. It was one of those indescribable spring days that can only be experienced in the Alps. I took in a deep breath of the cool, crisp air rushing in through the open window. The early morning sun was just beginning to reflect off the snow covered peaks surrounding our valley. The wild flowers strewn over the fields below were ready to burst into a riot of color . . . purple, yellow, blue, mauve.

I turned to look at my small son asleep in his crib, and felt the delicate movements of the unborn child within me. I was filled with warm emotion.

Slipping on my robe, I gently gathered my sleeping son in my arms. I found my mother, who had come to share this day with us, in the kitchen. She had already made the *cafe au lait* and was slicing the thick, Swiss bread. As we sat together sipping the hot coffee and eating bread smothered with rich butter and strawberry jam, I was overwhelmed with joy.

Mother reached into her pocket and handed me an envelope. I opened it and discovered her Mother's Day gift to me.

It seems but yesterday
you lay
new in my arms.
Into our lives you brought
sunshine and laughter—
play—
showers, too,
and song.
Headstrong,
heartstrong,
gay,
tend beyond believing,
simple in faith,
clear-eyed,
shy,
eager for life—
you left us
rich in memories,
little wife.
And now today
I hear you say
words beyond your years.
I watch you play
with your small son,
tenderest of mothers.
Years slip away—
today
we are mothers
together.
        Ruth Bell Graham

As I sat there beside my children in the pew, I couldn't help but reflect on how quickly the years had passed.

The small son I cradled that day is now a father with two little ones of his own. The unborn child that stirred

within me is now a happily married woman. Several brothers and sisters followed them. And now Mother and I are not only mothers together, but grandmothers together.

Children so quickly grow into parents, parents into grandparents, and grandparents into great grandparents. The role of parenting, I thought to myself, is like the ever-widening ripple a stone makes in the quiet waters of a mountain lake. Once you love, you are never free again.

I reflected on over twenty-six years of mothering, and I agreed with what John Trapp said many years ago: "Children are certain cares, uncertain joys."

I smiled to myself. Although the joys have far outweighed the cares and parenthood continues to be my most rewarding occupation, I do not find it easy. Parenting is a huge responsibility. It is demanding physically, emotionally, and spiritually. I thought of how Satan is attacking today's families. I thought back on the past year and how he had attacked our family. At times, the circumstances seemed overwhelming. But God, ever true to His Word, always provided the needed strength and promised wisdom.

My mother was once asked how she had raised five children with my Daddy being away so much of the time.

"On my knees," she replied.

Certainly I had not discovered a better or more effective way to raise children.

We are all parents together, striving to be faithful with responsibilities which God has entrusted to each of us. There are many times we feel overwhelmed, or become discouraged. But remember, God is a father with a mother's heart. When you feel depleted, simply turn to Him and exchange your insufficiency for His all-sufficiency.

With David we can say, "The Lord is my strength . . . my heart trusts in him, and I am helped" (Psalm 28:7).

Remembering

*Remember the days of old; consider the generations
long past. Ask your father and he will tell you,
your elders, and they will explain to you*
(Deuteronomy 32:7).

The fire crackled cheerily in the large fireplace, bathing my parents' living room in a soft glow. The only other lights were those from the tall Christmas tree which stood by the window. Snowflakes fell silently outside. I sat alone on the brightly polished hearth, hugging my knees and staring into the flames. Remembering . . .

This room with its beamed ceiling, ancient furniture, worn brick floor, and chintz-covered couches held so many memories for me. So much of what I knew of the Lord and the scriptures I learned right here.

Sundays were special growing up in this house. Mother woke us with gospel hymns playing on the record player and the smell of sweet rolls in the oven. After church and lunch, we rested, read, or took long walks to the top of the ridge, passing the "bears' den" on the way, or stopping by the reed field to gather wildflowers. Late in the afternoon my grandparents would arrive to spend the evening.

Our church did not have evening services, so we would eat a quick supper, then light the fire and gather in this room to sing hymns, play Bible games, and share experiences of God's goodness.

With my grandmother at the piano, we sang our favorites—from ancient hymns of the church to the popular new choruses. When our voices gave out, each child cuddled up to an adult who coached as we played "Spit In the Ocean" and "Twenty Questions." One by one, as the children grew sleepy, they were excused and tucked into bed, until only the older ones were left to listen as the adults reminisced.

Daddy might recount an exciting experience of God's faithfulness in his latest crusade, or tell how the Lord had led him in making a difficult decision. My grandfather, a surgeon, might tell how the Lord had touched a patient, bringing not only physical, but spiritual healing. Then a scripture or specific answer to prayer might be shared.

I grew up hearing of God's sovereignty, His constant presence, His protection and mercy, His power and grace, His faithful care and provision of both material and spiritual needs. My parents and grandparents always spoke of the Lord as they would of their best friend. These sessions were not planned, but flowed naturally and spontaneously from hearts filled with love and gratitude.

As I sat on the warm hearth recalling all the happy times experienced around this fireplace, I thought how precious is our Christian heritage . . . and how important it is to "remember." Scripture tells us to "remember what the Lord did . . . remember how he has led . . . lest you forget" (*see* Deuteronomy 4-6). I thought of what I wished to share of my own spiritual walk, which has taken me over hills and valleys, into delight and despair, fulfillment and frustration, success and failure. Often, I thought, my weaknesses have outweighed my strengths. At other

times, I have experienced supernatural courage and devotion. As I reflected on my life, I was aware how once again the Lord has used each weakness, each frustration, each failure to bring me into a closer relationship with Himself.

Yes, I had learned much in this beautiful little haven, surrounded by my family's love, secure in the faith of my parents and grandparents. Yet it has been during the darker, more difficult moments of later years, when I stood at the jagged end of my own strength, that the Lord has chosen to teach me the most enduring lessons . . . and the deepest experience of Himself.

I bowed my head before the embers of the ebbing fire. I thanked Him for lessons learned under the clear skies of a sunlit childhood. I also thanked Him for opportunities to prove His faithfulness in the long overcast days . . . and stormy nights.

Whatever the weather of your life, whatever your past, whatever your current experience, He is a shield of protection, and the source of strength and encouragement.

"But Thou, O Lord, art a shield
for me:
my glory, and the lifter of my head"
(Psalm 3:3, KJV).

My Father Loves Me

As a father has compassion on his children,
so the LORD has compassion on those who fear him
(Psalm 103:13).

T he mountains of North Carolina offer an ideal setting for the imagination of an eight-year-old to run wild.

The woods are full of places for small cowboys and Indians, riding magnificent stick horses and clutching homemade bows, to war with one another. (My "horse" was a palomino with a long, thick mane.) The soft green moss beneath a large oak became the sweeping lawn of an antebellum mansion where my sister and I could use our "dress-up" box and pretend to be grand Southern ladies. Or, if our mood and imagination so dictated, the scene could be transformed into a cozy cabin.

On the hill behind my grandparents' home just next door to ours was a special place we called "Fairyland." It was a secret spot, hidden from view by the thick bushes and undergrowth surrounding the knoll. A carpet of soft, deep emerald moss and several old trees with knotholes of every size and shape provided homes for all the fairies, gnomes, and elves that inhabited this enchanted hide-away. Even the various mushrooms made perfect tables and chairs just their size.

We loved to guess which old knothole housed the "tooth fairy" who faithfully placed a quarter or fifty-cent piece beneath our pillow each time any of us lost a tooth. How he managed to carry such a heavy object was beyond us! One night it rained and his feet got all muddy, for in the morning, there were tiny fairy footprints marching across the bed and pillow. (Mother also had a vivid imagination and artistic ability to match!)

I remember one clear, crisp day when we had been playing up behind our house. A large hollow stump, perched high above the road near a red clay bank, was our fort. We had stocked it with red clay balls (which, more than once, were tossed upon the unsuspecting cars below). On this particular day, I had been playing with friends and had been naughty—a fact that was causing my conscience to hurt badly. The more uncomfortable I became, the harder I played, trying desperately to ignore my conscience. I told myself that what I had done was really not so bad, and that, after all, no one would find out about it. But still I felt miserable.

Suddenly I heard the sound of a car, then commotion in my driveway below. When I heard my Daddy's voice, I froze. He had arrived home unexpectedly early. How ashamed I was! I felt cold, then hot. Of all people, I longed to please him. What should I do?

I ran as fast as I could down the hill into the waiting, loving arms of my father, with the assurance that, even if he did find out about my wrongdoing, he would still love me and forgive me.

Since that day so many years ago, I have often suffered from what George MacDonald calls "a conscience

doing its duty well, so that it makes the whole house uncomfortable." Though I may try to excuse or cover up my guilt, I am miserable until once again I remember that the only way to find peace is in the strong, loving, forgiving arms of my heavenly Father.

The Example

Spending the night at my grandparents' house was always a special treat. When I was all ready for bed, I grabbed my pillow and my school clothes, ran up our drive, crossed the little wooden bridge, darted across the street, and down into my grandparents' yard. The back porch light was still on, and I knew the door would not be locked.

When I ran in, LaoNaing not only gave me a hug, but some freshly baked custard and one of her hidden-in-the-cupboard mints. I kissed her good night, then circled through the living room to find Lao I. After giving him a kiss, I climbed the stairs to bed.

The small sleeping porch was perched high among the trees. With the bed pushed up against the windows, it was almost like being in a tree house. I loved falling asleep in the soft glow of the full moon.

Though I awoke early, the birds were up before me, singing their hearts out—blue jays, cardinals, thrashers,

Carolina chickadees, and, every now and then, a bright yellow-and-black Baltimore oriole or a vivid blue indigo bunting. Sometimes a woodpecker would drill just outside my window, waking me with a start.

The first rays of sunlight were just beginning to touch the ridge behind the house. I lay there watching as they gradually lit the summit, then slowly slid down the mountain. Before I left for school, the sun would have already reached the valley, warming us with its presence.

I could smell breakfast cooking—bacon, eggs, and hot biscuits! I got up and dressed quickly, then tiptoed down the stairs. When I reached the bottom landing, I peered around the corner into the living room. Yes, he was there as he was every morning, on his knees in front of the big rocking chair. I stood watching him until LaoNaing called us to breakfast. He got up slowly, rubbing his eyes before he replaced his glasses, his forehead still red and creased from the impact of his folded hands. He saw me and smiled. Giving me a warm hug and a big kiss, we went into the kitchen together.

I knew that this active surgeon, church layman, writer, former missionary to China, and family man had been up long before dawn, spending time with the Lord. He had an extensive prayer list, and I felt warm and secure, knowing he had already prayed for me. Now he was refreshed and eager to meet the rest of his busy day.

My grandfather never disappointed me as a man or as a Christian. Until the day he died, he set an example of balanced, fun-loving, disciplined, godly living.

When I examine my own life, I wonder what my children see. Do they see a concern for others, or do they see criticism, cynicism, and compromise? Do the things of eternal and spiritual value have priority in my life, or am I too preoccupied with the material and temporal things?

Which is more important—my children's little feet or their footprints? The fun we have eating popcorn together, or the salt and butter on the carpet? Do they discern a sense of peace and serenity in our home, or strife and tension? Do I walk my talk? Is there a noticeable difference in my life? Do they perceive acceptance, love, and understanding? Do they experience the results of my prayers? Is the fruit of the Spirit exemplified in my life?

Lord, "I will try to walk a blameless path, but how I need your help, especially in my own home, where I long to act as I should" (Psalm 101:2, TLB).

Most Important of All

He who is faithful in a very little thing
is faithful also in much
(Luke 16:10, NASB).

I t was one of those delightfully balmy days so typical of Florida. The doors of the classroom were open, allowing the soft breezes to blow the fragrance of orange blossoms through the room. I had arrived early and was sitting quietly at my desk, savoring the sensations of early spring. One by one the other students filed in and suddenly the shrill school bell sounded, interrupting my reverie and indicating the beginning of another school day.

We began class, as usual, with a brief devotional. I must admit I was distracted by the singing of the birds, the warm breezes, and the sweet aromas. I found it hard to concentrate—until something my teacher said caught my attention.

"The only thing the Lord requires of us," she was saying in conclusion, "is faithfulness."

Both excitement and peace flooded me at those words. There, sitting at my school desk in central Florida, a huge weight was lifted from my shoulders. Because, you see, even at my tender age, I had been feeling an awesome responsibility to "measure up." There was so much to live up to, so many big footsteps to walk in, so many examples to follow that I just didn't see how I was going to do it!

But—if the Lord's only requirement of me was faithfulness, then *He didn't expect me to be like anyone else!* And if the importance was in the faithfulness and not in the "greatness" of the task, then with His help I could serve and please Him in my own unique way. What a comfort! From that day on, my prayer was that no matter what He gave me to do—whether great or small, public or private—I would be faithful.

For me, faithfulness has meant staying up all night with a sick child, ironing my husband's suits when he forgets to take them to the cleaners, washing windows, pulling weeds. For others, it may mean remaining in a mundane or monotonous job or in a behind-the-scenes ministry.

Not everyone possesses boundless energy or a conspicuous talent. We are not equally blessed with great intellect or physical beauty or emotional strength. But we have all been given the same ability to be faithful. And, as we are told in the parable of the talents, it is the faithfulness that receives the commendation of God: "Well done, good and faithful servant! You have been faithful with a few things; I will put you in charge of many things" (Matthew 25:21).

Many years have passed since my teacher shared this simple truth with us, but it continues to be a source of encouragement to me even now. I still tend to compare myself to others and, sometimes, when I see those gifted Christians who seem to achieve so much for the Lord, I am tempted to admonish myself: *Gigi, if they can do it, so can you! After all, look at the advantages you have had!* Then I

recall that balmy day so long ago and hear Him saying to me: "I am not requiring all this of you. You have placed these pressures and expectations on yourself. I ask only that you be faithful."

The Same Spirit
Says the Same Thing

*Trust in the Lord with all your heart and lean not on
your own understanding; in all your ways acknowledge
him, and he will make your paths straight*
(Proverbs 3:5-6).

Daddy held my hand ever so tightly as we
climbed the steep, winding road to the little
church that clung to the side of the mountain overlooking
Montreux, Switzerland.

The jonquils nodded their heads approvingly as we
passed, and the yellow blossoms of the forsythia seemed
to have opened just overnight for us. The day had been
overcast with a drizzle of fine mist, but as we pulled up to
the church, the sun burst forth in celebration. Daddy gave
me one last, reassuring squeeze. We stepped into the
church and into a new life for me.

It was my wedding day.

As the soloist sang "Oh, Perfect Love," my thoughts
wandered to another mountain setting, only six months
before. . . . I was sitting on the window seat in my bedroom overlooking the Blue Ridge Mountains. The trees
were bare and the air so crisp and clear that I could dis-
tinctly see all the activity in the valley below. Bright

Christmas lights enticing shoppers. Cars winding slowly up the narrow mountain roads. Yellow-and-black school buses, stopping to unload children who were hurrying home to warmth and supper. And, every now and then, a long freight train inching its way lazily across the valley floor. Although I took note of all these familiar sights, my mind was thousands of miles away—high in the Swiss Alps.

In my lap was a letter from a handsome, godly man, six years my senior, who was asking me to marry him and move to Europe. Although I had met him several years earlier, I didn't know him well nor had we had any contact for many months. Yet, somehow, I knew the Lord was directly involved in this proposal. I glanced down and my eyes fell again on the sentence that kept turning over and over in my heart. It read simply: "The same Spirit says the same thing."

As I watched the late afternoon sun slide slowly behind the ridge, I wondered how a naive, seventeen-year-old girl could make such a momentous decision. I got up and walked to the bedside table where my Bible lay open to Isaiah 1:19: "If you are willing and obedient, you will eat the best from the land."

Was I willing? Did I really want God's will more than anything else in my life? Was I willing to be available to Him, to trust Him, to obey Him? Was I willing to follow His leading even if it meant leaving all that was dear and familiar to me and giving myself to a man I didn't yet know well enough to love?

I knew that I had to be able to answer these questions before I could know God's perfect plan for my life.

The days passed, and I continued to search my Bible and my heart. Then one day, I awoke with a real sense of joy. I knew beyond a shadow of doubt that I could answer

a resounding *yes* to each of those probing questions. Yes, I did want His will more than anything. Yes, I would follow and obey Him. Yes, I could trust Him. Hadn't He said, "For I know the plans I have for you . . . plans to prosper you and not to harm you, plans to give you hope and a future"? (Jeremiah 29:11).

The peace "that passeth understanding" flooded my being that December day, and I knew that the same Spirit that had impressed dear Stephan to ask me to marry him was now assuring me, by faith and not by feeling, to answer yes. . . .

My thoughts were suddenly brought back to the present moment by the majestic chords of the "Wedding March." I clutched Daddy's arm tightly as we walked down the aisle of that picturesque church. I heard him say, "Her mother and I do" as he answered the question "Who gives this woman to be married to this man?" and then I was exchanging rings with my new husband—rings in which were inscribed the words: "The same Spirit says the same thing."

He Is Coming!

*. . . While we wait for the blessed hope—the glorious
appearing of our great God and Savior, Jesus Christ*
(Titus 2:13).

"**M**ama, come quick! *Come quick!*" my young
son called excitedly, the cold winter air
rushing past the small snow-suited frame silhouetted in
the open doorway.

I ran to see what he wanted. He grabbed my hand
and pulled me into the fresh snow just beginning to melt
in the warm sunshine.

"There! *There!* Up in the sky!" he cried, pointing to a
bright object. With anticipation in his blue eyes and hope
in his voice, he asked, "Mama, is that Jesus coming back?"

Oh, how I wished I could have shouted a resounding
yes. Instead, I took the little fellow in my arms and
explained that it was just an airplane, reflecting the afternoon sun. Together we watched as the plane continued its
flight across the sky and over the mountain peaks.

As I rearranged his cap and adjusted his mittens, I
sensed a gentle rebuke in his disappointed face. I remembered

how I, too, had thrilled at the thought of the imminent return of the Lord Jesus. But I had become so caught up with the business of everyday living that I had lost my awareness of the reality that He could come back at any time.

The Scripture teaches that there is a special crown—a crown of righteousness—set aside for those who look forward to and love His appearing (*see* 2 Timothy 4:8).

Will He find me waiting, watching, ready?

* * *

It was Easter—my favorite time of year. I was visiting my grandmother and grandfather Graham in Charlotte, North Carolina, and woke up on Easter Sunday to the horrible realization that my mother had forgotten to pack a Sunday dress—much less a special one! I did the best I could. I wore an aqua skirt and a navy blue sweater that didn't match. When we arrived at church, there I was—the ugly duckling in the midst of all those beautiful Southern ladies and their daughters, dressed in their finest. I will never forget the terrible feeling of being so unsuitably dressed for that special occasion.

When the Lord returns, will we be awkwardly attired in our good works which are like filthy rags in His eyes? (See Isaiah 64:6.) Will we be wearing the old hand-me-downs of our parents and grandparents? Or the latest religious fashion? Or will He find us appropriately clothed in His righteousness alone?

"I delight greatly in the LORD; my soul rejoices in my God. For he has clothed me with garments of salvation and arrayed me in a robe of righteousness, as a bridegroom adorns his head like a priest, and as a bride adorns herself with her jewels" (Isaiah 61:10).

* * *

When I was a child, Daddy and Mother would often take the train from our small town in North Carolina to Washington, D.C., or New York. My sisters and I loved seeing them off at the train station and meeting them when they returned home. I can still feel the surge of excitement when I heard the whistle blow and knew the large locomotive was just around the last curve. Any minute now and I would see its big, bright light, and then I would be in my parents' arms again! But if I had been naughty while they were away, I felt self-conscious and embarrassed, knowing that a bad report of my behavior would bring them disappointment. Then I experienced not joy, but shame.

So it is with our Lord's return. Will He find us eagerly waiting, or will we be ashamed to see Him?

"And now, dear children, continue in him, so that when he appears we may be confident and unashamed before him at his coming" (1 John 2:28).

May the expectation of His coming not only bring joy and comfort to our hearts, but may this realization also purify our lives so that we will be ready . . . whenever. . . .

The Devil's Calling Card

I t was a lovely summer evening, warm and inviting, as we gathered for dinner out on the terrace. There was the usual noise and commotion around the table, with seven hungry children all clamoring to be served first and eager to relate their day's activities to their father who had just walked through the door.

As I reached for three-year-old Jerushah's plate, I realized she was whispering something under her breath. Leaning down, I heard her saying, "Peace and quiet. Peace and quiet." I asked who had peace and quiet. Lifting her big green eyes to me reproachfully, she replied, "Nobody has peace and quiet."

I felt rebuked. Once again I had overextended myself both physically and emotionally until I knew I was not exhibiting a peaceful, quiet spirit.

A few days later, I boarded a plane on my way to fulfill yet another commitment. Suddenly I felt myself shaking all over. The trembling was so violent that, for a moment, I thought I would break apart. I looked down, but there was no visible evidence of what I was experiencing. My hands were steady, and no one was staring at me. To those around me, I probably seemed the image of serenity. Yet I knew differently. I was exhausted and my inner reserves were depleted. I closed my eyes and cried out to the Lord. Then I heard Him say, *The journey is too much for you.*

I was reminded of another who long ago had found himself in a similar predicament.

Elijah had just experienced a tremendous victory (1 Kings 18-19). Now he was thoroughly drained in body and soul. The devil, who delights in attacking us when we're down, took full advantage of this situation to leave his calling card of discouragement at Elijah's door. Elijah was so disheartened that he said, "I have had enough, LORD . . . take my life" (19:4).

Flying at 33,000 feet above the earth, I felt much like this man of God—so discouraged I dreaded going on. I recalled how the Lord, in His infinite tenderness and mercy, had provided a prescription for discouragement. He recognized Elijah's fatigue and tenderly said, "The journey is too much for you."

He didn't scold or condemn Elijah. He didn't make him feel guilty or unworthy. Instead, because the Lord doesn't confuse physical weariness with spiritual weariness, He let Elijah sleep. While he slept, the Lord sent an angel to prepare a little meal, and after Elijah had been physically restored and refreshed, he was ready to receive some much-needed insight. The Lord showed him a great wind, an earthquake, a fire—but the Lord was not in any of these. After all the noise and commotion had died down, and the smoke and confusion had cleared, Elijah heard "a gentle whisper."

It was God.

Sitting on that plane, the Lord showed me that He was not to be found in a whirlwind of anxious activity, or in an earthquake of agitation, or in the fire of over-commitment and busyness that so quickly consumes—but in "gentle stillness." I felt His love and peace envelop me, and His strength continued to uphold me all the way home.

Nevertheless, some changes needed to be made in my life. Spiritually, this meant resting in His love, and spending more time in His presence.

Practically, I had to cut back on outside activities, saying no, even at the risk of being misunderstood. I took time to lie in the sun, read, enjoy my children, and sit quietly with Stephan in the evening. And you know, not only did I meet the Lord in this place of "gentle stillness," but I also discovered it was just where He had wanted me all along.

Missing Pieces

Though he stumble, he will not fall, for the LORD
upholds him with his hand (Psalm 37:24).

I looked out over the deep blue of the Caribbean, its mirrored surface broken only by an occasional sailboat gliding past. Stephan was swimming in the pool, his strong, sure strokes taking him back and forth in the cool water. How grateful I was for this time of rest and intimacy.

As I lay under the tropical sun, I recalled a story my mother tells of a man she once met while vacationing in this very spot.

He was an interesting and slightly eccentric character—an archaeologist with a passion for broken china. Most of us don't have much patience with such things, and broken dishes usually get thrown out with the trash. To this man, however, they represented a challenge. In fact, he had built an entire house from all the old discarded scraps and bric-a-brac he could find. And although it was quite a monstrosity, to his mind he had created a thing of beauty. He then sifted through the dirt around his home, collected bits and pieces of pottery and glass and patiently glued them back together.

Once, while visiting him, Mother asked if she might have a sample of his work. Delighted, he went to select one of his more "perfect" specimens. She said she would much prefer to have one that was cracked, marred—even incomplete. He looked puzzled.

"You see," she explained, "you remind me of God, who so carefully and lovingly takes the broken fragments of our lives and puts them together again. Here and there a piece may be missing—a death, a divorce, an accident, wrong choices. But God takes the pieces of our shattered lives and makes us whole and complete again."

I love that story, because I believe it applies to all of us. No one is perfect. We are all marred in some way. We have all failed, made mistakes, known defeat and disappointment. Many of us have been physically or emotionally crushed.

But God looks beyond our faults and sees our needs. Tenderly, patiently, He sifts through the debris, lifts His broken creature and brings healing and wholeness. And if a piece is still missing, His strength and love are sufficient.

His perfection meets the deep needs of our being. His completeness flows around our incompleteness and we are complete in Him (*see* Colossians 2:9-10).

Missing the Splendor

e sipped "Chocolate Viennios" at the cozy cafe in Solalex as we waited for the jeep that would take us up the mountain to Anzeindaz.

A few goats tugged at a large tuft of grass while the younger ones scampered nearby. Two enormous black pigs rooted in the barnyard of the chalet across the way. I wondered if they were fed the scraps of the thick bread, cheese, and sausage we had eaten earlier for lunch.

I glanced around at the indescribable beauty. Rocky alpine cliffs ascended sharply around us. The rushing stream, fed by melting snow and mountain springs, tumbled over large boulders nearby. Cows roamed freely in the gently sloping green pastures, their large cow bells clanging in what seemed a competitive chorus.

We heard the jeep approaching and quickly finished our hot chocolate. We jumped in while Mr. Giacomini filled the jeep with supplies he needed to take up with us. After all was loaded, he adjusted the four wheel drive, and we began our ascent.

I noticed a peculiar odor and glanced down at my feet. Sure enough, I had inadvertently stepped in a cow patty. I did my best to clean my shoe as I clung to the side of the jeep, trying not to bounce out while we twisted and turned our way up the rocky incline.

What a difference a few hundred meters make! Down in the valley it was pleasant, even warm. Here there was a definite nip in the air. I was glad I had brought my sweaters.

After about twenty minutes of bouncing on the hard metal benches, I glimpsed the gray slate roof of the refuge. It had been built low to the ground with deep eves as protection against the thirty or so feet of snow that covers this simple mountain shelter for about six months each year.

We entered the dining area and sat down at a long wooden table where we were quickly served hot tea, a local cheese and potato dish, salad, and Swiss bread.

After "tea" we went outside to enjoy the fresh air and the bleak beauty of early fall on these alpine slopes. Although it wasn't quite time for the snows to begin, we had the feeling they were not far away.

The rugged slopes, a riot of color in spring and a deep, rich green in summer, were quickly fading to brown. The cows stayed close by, instinctively knowing it wouldn't be long before they would be taken to lower pastures and placed into barns for the winter.

Few trees grow up this high—only shrubs and bushes dwarfed by the snows and wind.

As the afternoon progressed, the fog began to roll in over the mountains and descend in around us. Since the plan was to walk back to the village on foot, we knew we had better start our descent.

Pulling another sweater over my head and tucking my hands into my pockets, I hurried to catch up with

Stephan who had already started down the road. The cold air soon began to bite at my nose and ears, so I increased my pace to keep warm.

Several times I stumbled over a stone on the rough, rocky path. I caught myself, and began to pay more attention to the rocks and where I placed my feet.

But it wasn't long before I realized I was concentrating so much on the ground that I wasn't even looking at the majesty of the mountains . . . beauty such as I haven't seen before or since. I was so concerned about stumbling over the stones that I was missing the splendor of the scenery all around me. About halfway down the mountain, Stephan spied a mountain goat on the rocks high above us. I quickly looked up, but it darted behind a clump of bushes. I'd been watching my feet again and missed it. We didn't see another one.

I thought to myself, *How like my life.*

I so often find myself looking down, anxious and concerned over every little stone and obstacle in my life, that I miss the splendor and beauty around me.

I thanked the Lord for once again reminding me to "look up" and to "richly enjoy all that He has given me" instead of missing it or taking it for granted.

Like the loving touch of my husband's hand.

The billowy white clouds floating in a blue autumn sky.

The birds singing in the trees, and yes, even the funny, annoying little squirrel who sits in my birdfeeder hogging all of the birdseed.

The gentle snow flake grazing my cheek in winter.

The small arms of my grandchildren squeezing my neck.

The drawing by my first-grader which says, "Mom, I love you."

Yes, stones can be irksome and irritating. They can even cause us to trip or lose our balance from time to time. We may be bruised by inconvenience or strained with a bit of extra work. We may fall from our routine or blister because of an interruption. Our organized schedule may suffer a cut or scrape.

We may even have to walk through life a bit slower and choose our steps more wisely, trusting a little more in Him who keeps us from stumbling.

But it will be worth it. Because if we spend all our time anxiously looking down, watching for stones, we will surely miss the splendor.

And there are some things in life we may only see once.

Does God Like Me?

A gentle breeze dislodged a few delicate petals from the bougainvillea bush. They floated down beside my chair. I sat alone on my porch, savoring the cool morning air. It would be hot soon enough. A cup of coffee sat on the glass table beside me, and my Bible was open on my lap.

A pesky little squirrel sat in one of the large bird feeders stuffing himself while a mother duck and several ducklings hovered beneath him in anticipation that he would drop a few sunflower seeds their way.

I chuckled as I watched a huge toad cautiously hopping along the edge of the steps, keeping a watch out for Sidney and Jessica, our hefty rottweilers.

I closed my eyes, allowing the chirping birds and the wind rustling through the pines to soothe me.

I sat there contemplating all the beauty and evidence of God's love. The balmy breezes, the soft billowing clouds against a backdrop of brilliant blue, the lapping of the lake, the delicate scent of flowers, the birds, and yes, even the large toad and the selfish squirrel.

I have never really doubted that God loved me, but as I sat there alone, I began to wonder, *Does God like me?*

Would God want to sit here on my porch and have a cup of coffee with me?

Would God want to spend the day with me?

Would He enjoy being around me?

The more I thought of this the more I really wondered. I don't particularly like being with myself. I tend to be too high-strung, opinionated, and stubborn even for my own taste. I would not have chosen my particular personality or disposition, so why would God like me or wish to spend time with me?

I looked down at my open Bible, and remembered how He had sought out the company of Adam and Eve in the Garden. I thought of how He had walked with Enoch and Noah. How He talked with Moses. How He ate with Abraham and spent long afternoons with Mary, Martha, and Lazarus. I thought about how He sought out the company of the men on the road to Emmaus, and seemed to relish conversation with varied personalities and characters like practical Philip and thoughtful Nathanael.

Did He care about seeking me?

I took my Bible and began to read in the psalms. Soon my eyes fell on these words:

"He brought me out into a spacious place; he rescued me because he delighted in me" (Psalm 18:19).

Does God delight in me? Am I pleasing to Him? I thought of my own children. I love and accept them just as they are, all of the time, and this love and acceptance is in

no way based on their performance. But it is also true that I delight in them when they are *pleasing* to me.

I thought of how my children pleased me most. How delighted I am when they are obedient and faithful in carrying out their tasks and using their talents. How pleased I am when I see them being loving, kind, and forgiving to one another. How glad I am when I observe them growing in stature and increasing in wisdom and knowledge. How overjoyed I am when they choose to be with me and spend time with me.

I also thought of how it saddens me when they refuse to trust me. Or fail to show appreciation or do not use the gifts we have given to them. Or how grieved I am when they murmur and complain or take for granted all we do for them.

Could it be the same with God, my heavenly Father?

God loves me and accepts me at all times, but is He ever saddened by my forgetfulness or grieved by my ungratefulness? Is He ever displeased by lack of obedience?

The Scripture teaches that He is delighted with me when I am obedient. Samuel reminds us that obedience is even better than any sacrifice.

I was reminded of the parable of the talents and how pleased God must be when I am faithful with all He gives me and entrusts to me. I thought of how pleased He is when I follow His commandment to love Him with all of my heart, soul, and mind, and my neighbor as myself.

How glad He must be when He observes me growing in wisdom and overjoyed when I choose to spend time with Him.

Another bougainvillea petal fell softly upon the table and a big mother duck waddled past on the terrace. I

glanced at my watch and realized it was time to begin my day.

I leaned over and gently removed the soft pink petals from the table, and picked up the bag of birdseed to refill the almost empty feeders.

Yes, I concluded, as inconceivable as it seems, with all of my faults and imperfections, God not only loves me, but I believe with all of my heart He also likes me. He seeks my company. He wishes to walk and talk with me.

Thank you Lord, for this incredible fact. I feel so unworthy and yet so honored.

As I walked across the yard to the birdfeeder, I found myself humming the words of an old hymn:

> And He walks with me and He
>   talks with me,
> And He tells me I am His own.
> And the joy we share as we tarry there,
> None other has ever known.[1]

Note

1. C. Austin Miles, *In The Garden*, ©1912 by Hall-Mack Co. renew ©1940 by Rode Heaver Co., a division of Word, Inc.

The Valley

*But the land you are crossing the Jordan to take
possession of is a land of mountains and valleys*
(Deuteronomy 11:11).

Stephan and I finished our shopping and stopped for tea at Chez Manuel and La Place St. Francois. It was getting late. We would have to hurry if we were to arrive at the chalet in time for supper. When we left the city of Lausanne, however, we chose the small winding road that hugged the edge of Lac Leman instead of the freeway, sacrificing time for beauty.

The afternoon sun sparkled on the lake, dotted with small sailboats whose occupants were taking advantage of the warm days of late summer. The regal mountain peaks reflected in its deep blue stillness, and the large paddle boat, crowded with tourists, passed in an elegant silence broken only by the shrill whistle as it approached the next stop. The hills climbed sharply to our left, where many centuries of hard work had formed terrace upon terrace of neat vineyards. The vines were now laden with fruit soon to be gathered by the men and women who inhabited the ancient villages nestled on the hillsides overlooking the lake.

We drove through Vevey, then Montreux, where we had been married in the seventeenth-century church twenty years earlier. We passed the historic castle of Chillon, poised on the water's edge. Then, leaving the lake behind us, we entered the Rhone Valley where the soil is rich and black. Here there were not only vineyards, but orchards of apples and lush peaches, and fertile fields yielding an array of fruits and vegetables.

It wasn't long before we left the main highway and started up the steep, narrow, alpine road that would take us up and away from the valley floor. No longer did we see vineyards or orchards or fertile fields—only a small vegetable patch or flower garden here and there, and fields of hay, dotted with farmers cutting rhythmically with their long-handled scythes. Their wives, heads wrapped in brightly colored kerchiefs, raked alongside them.

We continued climbing, passing the old church of Huemoz where Stephan had been baptized as a child. We drove through our village, the steep road taking us past the chalet with dark green shutters where he had been born, higher and higher, until we reached our own chalet, clinging to the side of the mountain and nestled among the evergreen trees.

Our children came boiling out of the door, all vying for attention (and the candies they knew would be in our pockets).

Soon we sat down to a meal of Gruyére cheese, sausage, and thick Swiss bread. After supper I bathed the children and tucked them into bed. Then, going downstairs where all was quiet, I put water on for tea and lit the fire.

I sat gazing out over the valley below where we had passed only a short time before. Often it is obscured by

clouds and fog, but tonight the air was crisp and clear and the light from the full moon rising over the ridge bathed it in a soft glow. I remembered the clusters of ripening fruit, the orchards and fields almost ready for harvest. Then I looked past the valley to the French Alps beyond. They were magnificent. I could even glimpse Mount Blanc, the highest peak in all of Western Europe. Most of these mountains are snow-covered year-round, and I never tire of their awesome beauty.

Sipping my tea and watching the moon caress each peak as it rose higher and higher into the midnight sky, I thought of the mountains surrounding us, their steep ridges climaxing in sharp peaks just behind our chalet. They, too, were splendid, but with the exception of a few flowers and evergreen trees, barren and desolate. I thought of my life and how similar it was to these sur-roundings—its ups and downs, its mountains and valleys.

I have always dreaded the valley times, finding clouds and rain disagreeable and much preferring the warmth and brightness of the sun. I have striven for the mountaintop experiences, seeking to avoid the dense fog of struggle and pain.

The fire cast a cozy glow. As I finished my tea, I real-ized that although I had found exhilaration and excite-ment on the mountaintops, it was in the valleys that I had experienced real growth. It was there that the Lord had plowed, planted, pruned, and reaped a harvest in my life.

I sighed. In my spiritual selfishness, I loved the mountains. But the true test comes when we come down from the mountains. I longed to grow in Him and to bear fruit for His glory. So I bowed my head, thanking Him for mountain splendor, but also thanking Him for the valleys, willing now to accept them, submitting to the rain and fog, the plowing and pruning, knowing that He who plants the seed and tills the soil will bring forth fruit.

We see and experience the glory of God on the mountaintops . . . but we live it out in the valleys.

A Bunch of Busyness

I listened to the distraught voice on the other end of the phone.

Her plea sounded convincing. No, I didn't really have the time or strength to do what she wanted me to do.

But I heard myself saying, "Yes."

After I hung up, I looked at my calendar with disbelieving eyes. A couple of weeks ago, it had been blank. I had looked forward to a relatively quiet month. Now, as I glanced over the white squares, I noticed something marked for *every day of the month.*

Once again . . . I was overcommitted. How had it happened? Why do I find it so difficult to say no? Why do I feel guilty when I'm not totally busy?

I remember one occasion when I was rushing home from an all-day meeting to prepare dinner for my large family. One of the ladies in the car turned to me and asked, "And just what do *you* do to keep busy?"

I thought she was teasing. She wasn't.

With seven children, three dogs, and a busy husband, the answer should have been obvious. My immediate reaction was to laugh—but then I realized she was serious. I was grateful we were approaching her house so I could tactfully avoid a reply.

Being too busy has become a compulsion for many . . . and a way of life for most of us. We find ourselves "booked up" to the point that the truly important things of life—thinking, meditating, reading to a child, showing tenderness toward a mate, listening to a teenager, taking time to encourage a friend—have all but been lost. We even tend to view the overactive, overcommitted Christian as some kind of super-saint. Running around being busy has become synonymous with spirituality.

A friend of mine once commented that any activity not directly inspired by the Holy Spirit is just "a bunch of busyness." This is confirmed in Romans 12:1 (KJV), where we read that God wants us to be available to Him for "reasonable service." The word "reasonable" means "not excessive or extreme; moderate; possessing sound judgment" (Webster). This kind of service is holy and acceptable to Him.

Describing a woman of God, Proverbs 31:16 in the Amplified Bible puts it straight: "She considers a new field [of interest or activity] *before* she buys or accepts it— *expanding prudently* [and not courting neglect of her present duties by assuming others]. With her savings [of time and strength], she plants *fruitful* vines in her vineyard" (author's emphasis).

How can we avoid being bound by busyness? How can we learn and practice "reasonable service"? How can we protect ourselves from becoming overcommitted?

Another friend who teaches a Bible study found that

many of the women in her group were suffering from this common problem, and decided to teach them how to say no. One week she stood in front of the class and said, "It's simple. You put your tongue on the roof of your mouth, and you say *no.*"

A sensible, well-balanced life is a testimony to God's harmony.

Part Four
Into the Wind

The wind blows to the south
and turns to the north;
round and round it goes,
ever returning on its course.
Ecclesiastes 1:6

You know that the testing of your faith develops perseverance.
Perseverance must finish its work
so that you may be mature and complete,
not lacking anything.
James 1:3-4

The Reference Point

It was a lovely, sunny day at my parents' home in the mountains of North Carolina. Although it was bright and warm out on the front lawn, a persistent breeze kept disturbing the party decorations my two-and-a-half-year-old son and I had just placed on the little table. In a hurry to get ready for his little sister's first birthday party, we quickly rearranged all the brightly colored plates and cups—only to see them blow away again!

Little Stephan-Nelson was becoming increasingly agitated and impatient with this unseen enemy that kept threatening to destroy his sister's birthday party—not to mention all his hard work.

Suddenly, he darted out into the middle of the yard, lifted his little fist defiantly to the sky and shouted, *"Stop!"*

I often find myself feeling much as my small son did that day. The winds of change are blowing so strongly they threaten to destroy what I hold dear. I want to throw my arms up and shout, "Stop!"

A couple of years ago, an ad campaign promoting South Florida tourism used the slogan: "The rules are different here." Many of us parents could say that of the society in which we are trying to raise our children. We were raised with a different set of "rules"—a different value structure. Now we are faced with trying to bring up a family in a culture that scorns most of our moral values.

What should we as Christian parents do? What *can* we do? What should we teach our children about marriage and family? About commitment, honesty, and truthfulness? About respect and responsibility?

A few weeks ago, while halfheartedly watching television, I suddenly became intrigued by a news item. The commentator was reporting a growing concern that the young people of our country lack moral values. The government, he reported, was contemplating using the Bill of Rights in public schools to teach moral values, since schools are by law forbidden to teach religion. We seem to have lost our reference point.

I'm reminded of a true story about a bridge project in Pennsylvania. The highway department had crews working on each side of a river. As the workers approached the middle of the waterway, however, they realized something was terribly wrong. There had been a miscalculation, and the two ends would never meet! The reason? Each crew had used its own reference point.

What should be our personal reference point? Popular authors tell us we are our own gods and, "If it feels good, do it." Or they say that "looking out for number one" is our highest priority. Are secular values—so attractively packaged and marketed in the media and many of our schools—causing us to question our convictions? Do we compromise because "times have changed," or because "everyone is doing it"? Everywhere we turn,

we are told that no individual requires a reference point outside of himself. ("To each his own!")

Have you ever tried to drive on a highway without road markings? Not long ago, the North Carolina highway department was enlarging a stretch of interstate. For several weeks, there were no lines marking the different lanes. Numerous accidents and several deaths were attributed to the fact that there were no painted lines . . . no reference points.

If we're not alert and careful, we may be allowing our children to fix their minds and hearts on shifting, unstable reference points. That's as dangerous as driving down a black North Carolina highway at midnight with no centerline.

One mother asked, "Would you place your valuable antique vase or your jewelry box outside where it could easily be damaged or stolen? Of course not. And yet day after day we leave our precious children vulnerable to the damage and loss inflicted by godless influences."

As Christians, our reference point is the Bible. We must teach, both by instruction *and example*, that the Scriptures and Jesus Christ are our source of authority. All values, judgments, and attitudes must be gauged in relationship to *the* Reference Point!

This is best done by simply abiding in the Word of God ourselves . . . by letting our children see our love and respect for the truth of Scripture. We must let them observe us daily seeking our own direction and light from its pages. Then, slowly, little by little, we must lead them to seek answers to their own problems and questions, relying on the one *certain* reference point in a wildly changing world.

The Letter

uddenly it was quiet.

Amazing!

How can the fact of three children going out the door for school transform total chaos into calm?

I unloaded the dishwasher from the night before and straightened up the breakfast debris. As I filled the washing machine with dirty socks and shorts, I prayed the children would have a good day in school, and that their teachers would be given an extra portion of patience.

I poured myself another cup of coffee, and sat down to reread a letter I had recently received from a friend.

As I read, my heart went out to her.

Janet was a woman alone.

A few years ago, she and her husband of seventeen years divorced. Janet had moved with her husband from their small Northeastern town to a large metropolitan area. They settled away from all her family and had chosen not to have children. They both had good jobs, and enjoyed each other's company. They traveled, played golf, and took fun, spontaneous weekends together.

But somehow, the fun and laughter began to fade. Their life together began to sour, and after a few years of ups and downs, Janet's husband asked for a divorce. He soon remarried a woman with children and before long, he and his new wife had a son.

My friend remained alone.

Months passed into years and still she was alone. We did our best to include her in as many family activities as we could. Birthdays, Christmas, Thanksgiving, and summer vacations. We loved having her with us. The children thought of her as an aunt, and she contributed so much to our family although being around such a large, hectic household must not have always been easy for her.

Sometimes, after spending an afternoon in our home, she would call and admit that having her quiet, clean, house all to herself had its advantages.

But still, she was alone.

My eyes returned to the typewritten pages before me on the kitchen table. Although I often received cards and notes from Janet, this one disturbed me. I sensed a tone of bitterness and resentment. Bitterness over her divorce and settlement. Resentment of the new wife and baby. Anger and guilt over what she perceived to be her faults and failures in the marriage.

I was concerned. How could I help her?

Although I tried, I could not even begin to understand her situation. Yes, I had experienced times of loneliness, but nothing like the loneliness of rejection she was experiencing. How could I say to her, "Janet, I know just

how you feel," or, "I know what you are going through"? I knew that if she continued to harbor hurt, she would become deeply entangled in ropes of resentment. But I didn't think it appropriate to preach a sermon. How could I help when I had never experienced her pain?

I bowed my head and prayed.

I then opened the Bible and tried to think through my friend's situation from the Lord's point of view. What might He say to her in circumstances like these? After meditating on several passages, the following message of reassurance took shape in my notebook.

"*I know* her sorrows. *I am acquainted* with grief and *I am touched* by the feelings of her condition. *I myself have suffered*, being tempted so *I am able to comfort and support* those who are tempted. *I look down* from the height of my sanctuary, from heaven *I see and hear* the groaning of the prisoner."

Maybe I would never be able to completely understand her suffering, but He did.

Then I thought about the word prisoner. I have usually pictured someone behind bars, but did this term also fit her situation? Why yes, she was confined to conditions that she had not sought. And now she was in danger of becoming restrained and trapped by bitterness and resentment.

But the Lord went on to remind me He had come to loose the bonds and set the prisoner free.

So the best way for me to help her was to encourage her in Jesus Christ. Not by preaching but by showing His love, understanding, and compassion.

I longed to sympathize with Janet, so I decided to look up the word "sympathy" to see just what it really means. I was surprised to discover it had little to do with

having gone through the same experiences . . . but a lot to do with tenderness, kindness, acceptance, and compassion.

I asked the Lord to use me as His earthly instrument to show His love to her, realizing anew that He sees beyond our faults, and responds to our heart's deepest need.

As I got up to refill my coffee cup, I remembered a card tucked away in my desk drawer which read, "He cares. I hope that it helps to know that I do, too."

Perhaps a good place to begin would be to send it to Janet.

Devotions or Disaster?

I reached for the Bible story book, and handed it to Stephan. We had finally finished supper. The children were a little out of control, and I hoped that devotions would calm them down.

I'd cooked Stephan's favorite food: meatloaf and potatoes. But the children hate meatloaf and potatoes, so it's always a battle to get them to eat on meatloaf night. Ketchup was everywhere. The children did their best to disguise their dinner with the red stuff. I was relieved I had used the red placemats.

I glanced under the table and discovered Jerushah's poodle, Jeannie, enjoying rather large "crumbs" of meat loaf "accidentally" dropped during dinner, a tell-tale crimson mustache clinging to her white muzzle.

Aram had hidden a flattened potato underneath his paper napkin. I knew I should scold him and force him to eat it, but I just didn't have the strength. I decided not to notice.

Stephan opened the book and found the place in Samuel where we had left off the day before. The children were still giggling. Just as things began to quiet down, Antony yelled, "Mama, Tullian has his feet under my chair!"

"Tullian," Stephan said firmly, "sit up and put your feet on the floor under your own chair." Slowly, our teenager slid into a halfway upright position. I took Antony into my lap to keep him quiet as Stephan picked up the book to try again.

Before he got out even one sentence, the phone rang. All seven children—except Antony, who was in my lap and couldn't move—jumped up to answer it.

"Sit down!" said Stephan.

We let the phone ring. It stopped after eight or nine rings. Stephan tried again.

I glanced at the children. All of them, except the immobile Antony, had their arms and heads on the table with their eyes closed. I didn't want to interrupt Stephan for the third time so I snapped my fingers. They looked at me out of the corner of their eyes. I made eye signals that they were to sit up. Reluctantly they raised their heads and slumped back in their chairs.

Suddenly our large rottweiler, who had been sleeping lazily all day, lunged all one hundred thirty pounds at the glass door just behind Stephan's chair, barking as if there was no tomorrow. The children giggled.

Stephan stopped reading and we looked at each other in exasperation.

"It must be the devil," I said.

He ordered the dog to be still, shot a stern look at the children, and resumed the story of Samuel. He finally finished and started to ask the children a few questions.

"Who was Samuel's mother?"

"Hannah," answered one.

"Yeah, Hannah banana," interjected another. They all began to laugh. The dog launched into a fresh volley of barking and the phone rang.

Stephan gave up.

While not usually this disastrous, our family devotions are usually less than perfect.

I am often asked how we as a family have devotions. You can understand why I smile as I try my best to answer.

As a child, I grew up on family "prayers." Every day we gathered together after breakfast for a few minutes of Bible reading and prayer. Daddy or Mother would read a short passage of scripture and then lead us in prayer. This instilled in me the importance of family devotions because of the invaluable emphasis of focusing on the Lord as a family unit.

I am amazed to discover how few Christian families spend time together in prayer and Bible reading. Yet what a priceless experience it is to have one's parents share spiritual truths from the Word of God, and to hear one's mother or father asking God's blessing and protection on each one. If for some reason the father can't or won't practice this privilege and responsibility, then the mother should find an appropriate time to do so.

Perhaps because we have seven children with a twenty year age span, devotions have always been a struggle. Finding the time, discovering the best formula, and being patient and persistent and are all common problems associated with family devotions.

We have tried many formulas and devotional books. It's never been easy to find one that would challenge the

older children yet be interesting and understandable to the younger ones.

But we have discovered that devotions should be fun, and not boring. Holidays offer a good opportunity for variety. On Valentine's Day, for example, we may ask the children to recite a verse about love. This Easter their aunt placed different items from the Easter story in a basket. A nail, a crown of thorns, a piece of linen, a cross, etc. Then each one chose an item and read the appropriate scripture. This was meaningful as well as fun for all ages.

We try to accept that there will be distractions and interruptions.

We try to remember that children will not always be reverent.

We have not always been consistent, especially as the pace of life increases. *But we have persisted.* And we have begun to reap the rewards. We have seen our older children develop a love for the Scripture and a habitual reliance on the power of prayer. Those who now have homes of their own continue to have their personal family devotions.

Not long ago, Stephan saw one of our older sons walking in town with his fiancee. He asked him if they had been looking in the shops. "No," Basyle replied, "we've just finished having our devotions together in the car." One day over lunch, our eldest son, Stephan-Nelson, expressed to me how much family devotions had meant to him growing up. He said that our family times of focusing together on the things of the Lord had shown him that the Christian life was a daily, workable reality. Even though things got wild and hectic, he said, we didn't give up. Our family prayer times taught him that we persist because devotions are a *discipline*.

I was so grateful and realized that all the effort had been worth it. It also gave me the needed courage to continue the

struggle with the younger children.

Devotions can be a fiasco. But the important thing is not how perfectly they are conducted, or how theologically deep they are, but that the children sense the presence of Jesus in our homes and the *priority* that we as parents place on having a personal relationship with Him.

Even on meatloaf night.

How Do You
Find the Time?

t was such a beautiful day. I was working in
the yard planting flowers when I heard the
phone ringing. I put down my tools, chiding myself for
not having brought the portable phone outside with me.

I ran back into the house and grabbed the receiver,
my hands still covered with black soil, my sneakers leaving a trail of dirt behind me.

"Hello," I answered breathlessly.

"How in the world do you do it?" the voice asked me.

"How in the world do I do what?"

"How do you find time to be alone with the Lord?"
she pleaded. I finally recognized the desperate voice of a
friend in California. She went on. "My job . . . my home . . .
Bob . . . the children . . . they all demand my attention all
day—and much of the night as well."

I laughed in spite of my friend's frustrated tone, and

then began to share with her some of my own frustrations. It isn't simply a matter of finding the time, it's also a matter of finding the *energy*.

I told her about one young mother whose only quiet time with the Lord was in the bathtub, and that had to be late at night or the children would be clamoring at the door. I shared with her the experience of another friend, the mother of three toddlers, who finally got so frustrated trying to read her Bible in peace that *she* crawled into the playpen.

There are no easy answers, no quick solutions, no ideal circumstances for moms with small children trying to find time for personal devotions. I used to have this idealistic vision of spending hours on my knees, of having long, involved Bible studies, of becoming a Truly Spiritual Woman.

Then I had children.

After over two and a half decades of parenting, you'd think I would have found a formula, or discovered the secret of having perfect personal time with the Lord.

I wish I did have a simple solution. But I can only share what I have learned—along with the struggles and obstacles I still encounter.

The first thing I discovered is that *you will never find the time . . . you have to take the time.*

Over the years, I have explored different ways of "taking the time" to be with the Lord. I have tried getting up early, but with new babies needing to be fed and small children having nightmares you already feel robbed of precious, much-needed sleep, and it doesn't take long for exhaustion to take over. I have tried meeting the Lord at night, when all was quiet except for the hum of the refrigerator and the rhythmic ticking of the grandfather clock.

Always a night person, I savored this time, and it worked for awhile. But then as my days became longer and my responsibilities greater, I would often crawl into bed too exhausted to think, much less read my Bible and pray.

I experienced a lot of frustration . . . and quite a bit of guilt. Then one day I realized I had been looking at this problem all wrong. The Lord had blessed me with these responsibilities, so couldn't He meet me right in the middle of my duties and obligations?

My mother had five children and didn't often have time for long devotions. But I can remember her Bible always open in a convenient place—the kitchen counter, her bedside table, beside the sofa, or even on the ironing board. In this way, she could quickly glean a promise or memorize a verse as she continued her work.

Following her example, I often pray for each child as I iron a dress or fold a shirt. I find myself thanking the Lord for their healthy little bodies as I bathe them at night. I praise the Lord for their beds and hot running water as I change their sheets and scrub the tub.

I find I can worship Him as I sweep the terrace, or trim the hedge, or dust the living room. I can meditate as I take a walk or rake the leaves. I have discovered that spiritual growth is not dependent on the length of time we spend in formal worship, but often comes through small visits with my Lord.

These brief snatches of spiritual refreshment have often served as my spiritual lifeline. On days when things seem to be going from bad to worse and my nerves are stretched to the limit and I feel myself drowning in mass confusion, slipping off for five minutes with the Lord buoys me up like a life preserver. Isaiah puts it this way, "In repentance and rest is your salvation, in quietness and trust is your strength" (Isaiah 30:15).

I often find it helpful just to sit with my hands open in my lap in an attitude of expectation. I may read a passage of Scripture or meditate on a single verse, such as Isaiah 41:10: "So do not fear, for I am with you; do not be dismayed, for I am your God. I will strengthen you and help you; I will uphold you with my righteous right hand." I simply receive His love, feel His presence, accept His strength, claim His promises, and then go back to whatever I was doing with renewed courage.

Brother Lawrence, a seventeenth-century monk, developed a deep and rich spiritual life by "practicing the presence of God." This meant he was conscious that God was with him each and every moment. His simple philosophy, set forth in the little classic, *The Practice of the Presence of God*, has been a great source of encouragement to me. Brother Lawrence's responsibilities were not in the pulpit, nor in the prayer chapel, but in the kitchen. He wrote, "The times of business does not with me differ from the time of prayer; and in the noise and clatter of my kitchen, while several persons are at the same time calling for different things, I possess God in as great tranquility as if I were upon my knees at the blessed sacrament."

What a lovely relationship! What a precious friendship! True spiritual intimacy is when we come to the place where the Lord is so much a part of our lives that we experience His presence with us in every activity, every duty.

Paul encourages us in 1 Thessalonians 5:17 (KJV) to "pray without ceasing." I don't think he was admonishing us to stay on our knees twenty-four hours a day, but to be in an attitude of open communication with the Lord. Who better than a busy mother could relate to prayer without ceasing . . . without ceasing our work? We would seldom pray if we could not pray while nursing a baby, bathing a toddler, washing dishes, or chauffeuring children back and forth to school.

Small snatches of spiritual refreshment do not replace the need for careful, in-depth Bible study. Some time, even an hour a week, or two half hours, should be set aside for more concentrated, profound study if we are to grow spiritually. Peter tells us that grace and peace come with an increased *knowledge* of the Lord Jesus, and that He has given us everything we need for life and godliness through our knowledge (2 Peter 1:3). This knowledge comes through the study of His Word.

I have discovered that devotions and Bible study are a discipline, and sometimes, if we are honest, we allow our busy lives and hectic households to be excuses for our own lack of organization and discipline. It takes an effort to put our chores aside for an hour, or get out of bed thirty minutes earlier.

One night the children and I watched a television program called "The African Water Hole." This program showed all the activities around a water hole in the African bush in midsummer when water is scarce. The need for water was so great the animals literally risked their lives twice a day when they approached the water hole to satisfy their thirst in the presence of their predators.

Our souls thirst for God, "the living God," yet how much are we willing to risk or give up in order to drink of the living water and grow deeper in the things of the Lord? Are we willing to discipline our lives? Give up a few hours of television? Unplug the phone? Forgo a shopping trip?

Often our busy lives lead to physical and spiritual weariness. "My soul is weary," Job cried, and I am sure there are times when each of us can echo his words. But, the Lord Jesus Himself provided the antidote when He said, "Come to me, all you who are weary and burdened, and I will give you rest . . . you will find rest for your souls" (Matthew 11:28-29).

How do we find the time?

"Reverence for God adds hours to each day" (Proverbs 10:27, TLB).

Pass It On

*When a good [woman] dies, [she] leaves
an inheritance to [her] grandchildren*
(Proverbs 13:22, TLB).

She looked so small and frail sitting on the edge of her bed. Snowy white hair framed her sweet face which, although lacking its usual color, was nonetheless radiant with peace and joy. Her tired, sunken eyes were still full of love and concern for each one who entered her room. In the last weeks of her life, she spoke often of the wonderful Christian heritage that had been hers and of her great privilege in passing that legacy on to her children and grandchildren. Her joy was complete, for all of her family loved the Lord Jesus.

As we approached her bedside, she somehow found strength that was not hers. Taking each one in her arms, she gave us a special verse or a personal blessing. Then, with deep conviction in her weak voice, she said, "Pass it on. Pass it on."

A few days later, Grandmother Graham died.

God in His sovereignty chose to place me in a Christian home, through which I received a godly heritage from both sides of the family. The privileges and responsibilities of passing on such a heritage are enormous. The Bible says, "To whom much is given, much is required."

Like a pebble thrown into a quiet lake, the ripples caused by the initial seed of godliness planted in a family and cultivated by the Holy Spirit become larger and broader, encompassing an ever-widening expanse. The cycle will continue, as long as we who have received such a heritage are faithful in our own personal walk with Jesus Christ and to our God-given responsibilities in our homes.

Think for a moment of how many people could be influenced by just one child reared to love and serve the Lord Jesus—a child who has been grounded in God's Word and has been given the examples of godly parents. The potential of faithful, God-fearing parents is unending. That very thought should cause us to reverence our job and be grateful to God for the great privilege He has entrusted to us.

If you have not been blessed by a godly heritage, you have a great opportunity before you. You can *begin* such a heritage for your children and grandchildren by making sure of your own relationship to Jesus Christ—and faithfully passing it on.

"The Lord himself is my inheritance. . . . He guards all that is mine. . . . What a wonderful inheritance! I will bless the Lord" (Psalm 16:5-7, TLB).

The Devil
Is a Good Devil

The long antique table was set with our best silver and china, its polished surface reflecting the warm glow of candlelight.

It was unusual for us to be gathered in the dining room for our evening meal. We usually ate supper in the cozy kitchen around the big, circular lazy-Susan table in front of the fireplace. (Each of us would hold onto the lazy-Susan and, as soon as the blessing was over, we would see who could be first to spin it. Mother used to say this prepared us for life in a highly competitive world!)

However, since Daddy was home from a crusade, we had decided to celebrate his homecoming.

Daddy said the blessing, ignoring the baby who kept interrupting with his "Amen." Then, minding our manners, we passed the Southern-fried chicken, homemade rolls, rice and gravy, and for dessert, Bea's* famous apple pie. How nice it was to be a complete family again. How glad we were that Daddy was home.

---

* Our long-time housekeeper.

At mealtime fun and laughter abounded, and during dinner someone began to sing a chorus that was popular in the 1950s.

> I've got the joy, joy, joy, joy down in my heart.
>   (Where?)
> Down in my heart—down in my heart.
> I've got the joy, joy, joy, joy down in my heart,
> Down in my heart to stay.
> I've got the love of Jesus, love of Jesus
>   down in my heart.
>   (Where?)
> Down in my heart—down in my heart.
> I've got the love of Jesus, love of Jesus
>   down in my heart.
> Down in my heart to stay.

Soon, we all joined in and continued through several more verses, concluding with our favorite.

> And if the devil doesn't like it, he can sit on a tack.
>   (Ouch!)
> Sit on a tack—sit on a tack.
> And if the devil doesn't like it, he can sit on a tack.
> Sit on a tack to stay.

To our great surprise, Daddy looked up with a frown and said sternly, "I don't want you to sing that verse anymore."

We were taken aback, since he was on old softie and tended to spoil us. We all looked at him.

"Why, Daddy?"

"Because," he replied, "the devil is a good devil."

All of us—including Mother—burst out laughing. Then we noticed he looked very serious and the laughter died away.

"What I mean," he explained, "is that the devil does a very good job being a devil, and I think it is wrong to take him lightly or mock him. He is real and powerful, and he is no joking matter."

I sat there pondering what Daddy had said. I didn't understand fully at the time, but I began to develop a healthy respect for Satan and the power he wields. And though I have never been afraid of him, knowing I am under the protection of the blood of Jesus, neither have I given him the satisfaction of being preoccupied with him. Following Daddy's advice, I have never touched those things associated with Satan's domain. Years later, when the occult and witchcraft began weaving its way through our popular culture, I asked the Lord to help me be sensitive and discerning concerning these matters, whether it be a book or a movie or a careless joke or conversation.

A sober warning at the dinner table so many years ago seems wiser than ever.

I Remember a
September Day

The suffocating September heat and humidity of central Florida greeted me as I climbed from the car. Sand immediately filled my shoes, and gnats swarmed around my face. But as I looked around, I forgot my discomfort.

I had never seen anything quite so lovely.

The old Spanish estate was set in the midst of four hundred acres of semitropical gardens and orange groves. Huge oaks laden with Spanish moss lent an almost exotic flavor. The large, red-tiled mansion was graced by court-yards, formal gardens, fish ponds, colonnades, and a sweeping lawn that sloped gently down to a quiet lake.

I strolled around the grounds, trying to acclimate myself. It was like walking through one of the popular romantic novels girls of my age so loved to read. My emotions were mixed. I had wanted to come here, but beautiful as it was, it was not the setting for a romantic novel, nor was I the heroine of a make-believe plot.

This was real. And the reality of it sent a strange feeling rushing to the pit of my stomach. In just a few minutes, my family would climb back into the car, leaving me here alone. And with the exception of Christmas and summer vacations, this lovely, strange place would be "home" for the next four years. Not yet thirteen years old, I was going to boarding school for the first time in my life.

My family hauled trunks and suitcases up to my room. We held hands, embraced, shed tears . . . and then said goodbye. Then they left, taking with them all of my courage, self-confidence, and joy, and leaving me with a terrible sense of loneliness.

It was my first period of true testing. It was time to put into practice everything I had learned. Now was the time to try God, to prove Him true to His promises, to place my total trust and confidence in Him alone, to learn to cast all my anxieties upon Him. Now was the time to discover the reality of His presence. To find out for myself that He really did care about me, Gigi, as an individual. To rest in the truth that I was His personal concern, and that nothing is too big or too small to escape His notice.

That was many years ago, but I have never forgotten the lessons I absorbed in those four years. The Lord Jesus became my Best Friend. I learned to rely on Him, and to this day He has never once failed me nor disappointed me.

When we are in a situation where Jesus is all we have, we soon discover He is all we really need.

It Mattered Less Than Love

ne day while discussing the subject of love, I asked my children for their definition of marriage. One of my little boys piped up and said, "It's when you find someone you want to keep!"

Stephan and I entered marriage with a firm conviction that it would be a lifelong commitment—not just a convenience held together by contract. We began our union on a solid foundation of shared faith, love, and a mutual desire to glorify God. But that doesn't mean it has always been easy or smooth. We've had our share of struggle and conflict.

Stephan is from an Armenian-European background, and I, from a small Southern town in the United States. Married in Switzerland, we made our first home in one of its lovely valleys—very romantic, especially when the full moon would slide up from behind the mountains. But even this fairy-tale setting could not ease the adjustments between two such different persons.

There were so many cultural shocks and hurdles to overcome. I didn't speak a word of French at the time, and with family and friends thousands of miles away, it wasn't long before I became lonely and homesick.

I discovered early on that the honeymoon high was not destined to be a steady marital experience but that reality demanded the unique blending of two distinct individuals from widely differing backgrounds and contrasting cultures. Difficulties were sure to arise; misunderstandings would become full-blown arguments; feelings would be hurt. But with each disagreement I found myself more determined than ever to develop, deepen, strengthen, and encourage our love and commitment to each other.

Someone has said that true marriage is not without conflict, but is ever resolving its conflict. This will mean determination, understanding, seeing things from the other's point of view, humility, being willing to be the first to say, "I'm sorry."

Many years, seven children, and innumerable arguments later, I can assure you that it's worth it!

> I do not say that there were no
> Misunderstandings, discontents,
> And hurts. I would it had been so.
> Strange how the heart sometimes assents
> To angers that the will asserts.
> But these we learned to live above.
> I do not say there were no hurts.
> I say they mattered less than love.[1]

Note
_____

1. Jane Merchant, *Halfway Up the Sky*, Abingdon Press, 1957.

The Green Ribbon

It was Saturday, Israel's day of worship. Stephan, the children, and I decided to drive out of the city and into the hills around Jerusalem. They are rugged and barren—beautiful in an almost mystical sort of way. We never tired of exploring them.

After stopping at a small cafe for *pita* and *falafel*, we found ourselves on the old dirt road that winds through the wilderness from Jerusalem down to the plains of Jericho. We pulled the car over to look at the ancient hills of Moab silhouetted against the eastern sky, and to watch the afternoon shadows playing eerie games of hide-and-seek with the deep ravines and steep precipices.

As I stood gazing at these ancient hills and soaking up their mysterious beauty, my eyes fell on a ribbon of lush greenery. It was so out of character, so cool and inviting in the midst of the heat and dust of the desert. I realized with a start that here, in the middle of the wilderness, there must be an underground stream, providing nourishment and refreshment to the trees whose roots were firmly embedded along its banks.

Immediately Psalm 1:3 came to mind: "He is like a tree planted by streams of water, which yields its fruit in season and whose leaf does not wither. Whatever he does prospers."

How encouraging that even in times of dryness, even when I go through a desert experience, I can flourish and bear fruit if I am deeply rooted in the Source of living water.

Root yourself deeply in Him . . . so that you may never forget that you are only the channel. He is the Source.

The Kiss

As soon as we heard the news that LaoNaing had suffered a stroke, we caught a plane to North Carolina. Arriving in Asheville, we went directly to the hospital, where we found my maternal grandmother lying frail and helpless, attached to life-sustaining tubes and machines. We could sense her frustration and agitation. Although she could not speak, she made it known in no uncertain terms that she wished to go home.

After consulting the doctor, we decided to comply with her wishes. As soon as she saw the familiar surroundings and was tucked safely in her own bed, she relaxed, and a peaceful expression replaced the one of strain and concern. We kept her as comfortable as possible and, knowing she enjoyed our presence, someone always kept her company as well.

Since LaoNaing had loved music all her life, Mother had a special tape made for her—hymns that would especially bless and encourage. Since my grandmother was aware she was dying, the hymn she wished to hear over and over again was "The King is Coming."

Each day she grew weaker. It was hard to see her fading slowly away, but she was ready and eager to meet her Lord and to rejoin loved ones who had gone before.

She died early one November morning—quietly and peacefully.

When I went to tell the children, little Tullian said, "Mama, LaoNaing had a hurt, and Jesus came and kissed it away." This two-year-old understood better than I the "homegoing" of a child of God. Thinking I was offering comfort, I found myself comforted.

I do not know when the Lord will come for me. I may live to a ripe old age like my grandmother, or He may choose to complete my life early. But I do know that He has provided for my eternal security through Jesus Christ and that until that day, He provides for my daily life through the power of the Holy Spirit.

> As the portrait is unconscious
> of the master artist's touch,
> unaware of growing beauty,
> unaware of changing much,
> so you have not guessed His working
> in your life throughout each year,
> have not seen the growing beauty
> have not sensed it, Mother dear.
> We have seen and marveled greatly
> at the Master Artist's skill,
> marveled at the lovely picture
> daily growing lovelier still;
> watched His brush strokes
> change each feature
> to a likeness of His face,
> till in you we see the Master,

feel His presence, glimpse His grace;
pray the fragrance of His presence
may through you seem doubly sweet,
till your years on earth are ended
and the portrait is complete.
                    Ruth Bell Graham
                    (Written for her mother.)

The Rock

I sat upstairs by my bedroom window, reading and enjoying the spectacular view—brilliant red and gold fall foliage against a crisp blue sky. A faint scent of burning leaves drifted in through the open window, reminding me it would soon be time to rake our yard.

Back from school, the children had quickly changed their clothes and rushed back outside to spend the rest of the afternoon playing football just beneath my window. I watched them with pride and joy, thanking the Lord for their healthy minds and bodies.

Then I noticed my oldest—limping. A blister, maybe? I made a mental note to ask him later.

The shadows lengthened, and the air turned cooler as the late afternoon sun began its descent. I grabbed a sweater and went downstairs to begin dinner.

When the children came in to wash up for supper, I

noticed my son still limping—now rather badly.

"What's wrong with your foot?" I asked.

"Oh, nothing," he shrugged. "I just have a rock in my shoe."

"Well you've been limping all afternoon! Why don't you take the rock out?"

"Because I put it there to remind myself to be nice to Basyle."

I quickly turned my head to hide my amusement. But I had to admit he had a point!

We may not need to put a rock in our shoe, but we can ask the Holy Spirit to make us more sensitive to His gentle reminders, taking more time to be quiet before Him, listening to Him. Perhaps the voice of the Lord will come through a friend. Or one of the children. Or a message. Or a book. But more often it is through His Word and in prayer that we hear His still, small voice. He speaks to us when we fall short, and then brings encouragement, promising to give us the wisdom and strength to grow more and more like the person of Jesus Christ.

Do you have a rock in your shoe today? Rather than limping through your routine, why not stop and check it out. It may be there for a good reason.

Holy Audacity

Family, friends, and dignitaries—including the President of the United States—had gathered to show their love and respect for Daddy, who was being honored in Charlotte, North Carolina.

Members of the immediate family were seated close to the front, behind a roped-off area. Security was tight. Uniformed police and Secret Service agents kept a watchful eye on the crowd. An air of excitement hung over the auditorium in anticipation of the president's arrival. Suddenly there was a flurry of activity as he entered, surrounded by his associates and bodyguards.

So intent were we on watching the proceedings that none of us noticed when four-year-old Basyle dashed under ropes and past the policemen and agents. Running directly to the president, he tugged on his sleeve. Startled, the man looked down into the small, eager face.

"Are you the president?" asked Basyle.

Graciously, the great man assured him that he was.

Amused and embarrassed, we retrieved our young son. Several times during the program, Daddy and the president glanced down toward Basyle and chuckled.

Later, however, as I reflected on the incident, I couldn't help admiring the audacity of my four-year-old boy. I compared it with my own often timid approach to the King of kings and Lord of lords.

We are directed to "approach the throne of grace with confidence," yet, for various reasons, I hesitate. There is only "one mediator between God and men, the man Christ Jesus" (1 Timothy 2:5). No ropes, no police, no Secret Service. Yet I allow the smallest obstacle—busyness, haste, world distraction—to hinder my entrance into the Most Holy Place.

Prayer has no boundaries except my failure to accept the open invitation to the throne of grace. I humbly acknowledge that, more often than I care to admit, my problem with prayer is prayer*less*ness, caused by my frustration over circumstances . . . and my lack of audacity in approaching the King of kings.

"For we do not have a high priest who is unable to sympathize with our weaknesses, but we have one who has been tempted in every way, just as we are—yet was without sin. Let us then approach the throne of grace with confidence, so that we may receive mercy and find grace to help us in our time of need" (Hebrews 4:15-16).

Too Loved to Leave

y life seems characterized not so much as a "pilgrim's progress," but as a "struggler's struggle."

Have you ever felt you have disappointed the Lord so often that you don't see how He could love you?

Have you ever been so discouraged that you contemplated giving up?

Have you ever thought, "It just isn't possible for me to live the Christian life"?

Well, I have.

Fortunately, the Lord is good, ready to forgive, full of compassion, and gracious (Psalm 86:5,15). And He has His own unique ways of reminding us that we are His and that He does love us.

Not long ago I met one of those rare individuals whom you recognize as a Christian by the expression on his face. His bright, contagious smile was only a reflection of a warm, loving personality. As he walked into the room and introduced himself, his whole being radiated Christ. But it had not always been so, as he explained to me one day.

A few years before, this man had accepted Christ as his Savior. Once he made his decision, he became an enthusiastic believer. His wife, however, just couldn't follow him in his new-found faith. So, after a couple years of struggle, she asked him for a divorce. Since he had become so involved in his faith, she explained, their lives had "drifted apart."

"Okay, honey," he said kindly. "You go ahead and file. But I want to warn you that no court in the country will grant you a divorce."

Taken aback, she asked him why.

"Because," he replied with a twinkle in his eye, "no judge will grant a divorce to a woman whose husband loves her as much as I love you!"

She did not go through with the divorce. And not long after this experience, she, too, was drawn to the Lord.

So it is with the Lord's love for us. His commitment to us is total and irrevocable. He loves us far too much to stop now.

Even when we don't follow Him.

Even when we drift from Him.

Even when we become so discouraged that we just can't go on.

At such times we may feel His arms around us, drawing us into the stillness of His chambers (Song of Solomon 1:4) and leading us to the banquet hall (2:4), where we can feast on His encouragement and acceptance, and hear Him say, "I have loved you with an everlasting love; I have drawn you with loving-kindness (Jeremiah 31:3).

"I'll Be Dogged
If I Will"

A unt Cecile was a feisty little lady who lived a few houses from us when I was growing up. She had soft white hair which framed her angelic face, and a laugh that was contagious. Everyone loved Aunt Cecile and enjoyed being around her. I especially found in her a kindred spirit. I appreciated her zestful approach to life, and her honest, down-to-earth way of expressing herself.

She had raised her family of six children in Korea where she and her husband served the Lord as missionaries. On top of her mission duties, and those of wife and mother, she also played the piano for the church services.

One Sunday morning, after getting her brood fed and dressed for church, she was exhausted. She sat down at the piano waiting for the hymn number to be announced. The pastor rose and said, "Mrs. Coit will now play 'Oh, Sweet Day of Rest and Gladness.' "

Aunt Cecile got up slowly from the piano bench, looked the pastor straight in the eye, and said emphatically,

"I'll be dogged if I will." With that, she sat down.

Not long ago, I had one of "those" days.

I had worked hard, been interrupted umpteen times, settled scores of arguments, and tried to be sweet and patient even though I felt anything *but*! After dinner I was cleaning the top of our glass dinner table (a dumb table to have with seven children) and, all of a sudden, everything got to me. The grease spots on the table, the kids fighting, the phone ringing, the teenagers talking, the TV—everything! I threw down the towel, and ran to my room in a flood of frustrated tears, declaring as I went, "I quit!"

As much as I love and enjoy my calling of wife and mother, I would not be honest if I didn't admit there are days when enough is enough. I want to put my hands on my hips and declare, "I'll be dogged if I will!"

So I have to run to the Lord and pour out my honest feelings. I don't try to hide from Him my anger or self-pity or frustrations. He knows all about them, anyway.

> *Would not God have discovered it,*
> *since he knows the secrets of the heart?*
> (Psalm 44:21)

I simply tell Him when I feel misunderstood, when I don't have strength for all the demands placed on me, or when I feel insignificant or taken for granted. Like David, I confess that I am overwhelmed (Psalm 61:2). And though it is often the trivial things that overwhelm us, the Lord knew there would be such days, and "daily bears our burdens" (Psalm 68:19) without ever condemning or comparing our seemingly insignificant trials with those unbelievable burdens other dear ones are called upon to bear.

Whatever size the trial, whatever the weakness, He is our inexhaustible source of strength.

Even This?

My God in His lovingkindness will meet me
(Psalm 59:10, NASB).

Though early morning is not my best time of day, after a couple cups of coffee, I managed to fix breakfast, wash the dishes, and usher seven children out the door to school before heading for the laundry room.

I stopped abruptly at the door, gazing in disbelief at a mountain of dirty clothes that represented a minimum of three loads of wash. Hadn't I just washed three loads yesterday? Sudden tears of frustration stung my eyes. I quickly brushed them away, ashamed of myself, and put the first load in the washer.

Then I continued to tidy up, picking up the morning newspaper and various cups and glasses left from snacks the night before. Wiping a fingerprint here and there, I straightened beds and collected odd socks and shoes, school papers, and books. Soon I found myself in my son's bathroom, scrubbing the tub. Once again the tears insisted on imposing themselves against my will.

This time they found little resistance.

I was frustrated and discouraged, and my self-esteem was about as low as it could get.

It was still morning, but I was tired—weary of the mundane routine that made up my day and characterized much of my life. I was tired of the same mess day after day—of washing clothes that only yesterday I had folded and returned to their proper places; of wiping sticky fingerprints from the windows and mopping the same floors again and again; of doing the dishes, only to get them out a short time later to reset the table. I was sick of spending hours cooking a meal that was consumed in minutes.

Sitting in the middle of the bathroom floor, sponge and cleanser in hand, tears streaming down my cheeks, I found myself crying and praying all at the same time.

God, in His lovingkindness, came to meet me. Quietly and clearly I heard Him say, *Whatever you have done for one of the least of these . . . you did for me* (Matthew 25:40).

"Lord . . . even this?"

Especially this. Who else is going to do it for Me? In all these small ways, you are serving Me.

Reassured and encouraged, I dried my tears and continued to scrub the tub . . . for Him.

One Step at a Time

he cog railway car groaned and moaned as it began an arduous ascent up steep tracks.

The day was perfect. Not a cloud in the deep September sky. The air was warm with just a hint of fall.

As the train snaked its way slowly out of the village and began its climb up the mountain, I looked out the open window at the quaint beauty of Switzerland. We passed children in bright-colored sweaters running home for lunch, rosy-cheeked women hanging their laundry out in the fresh air to dry, or trudging home with baskets full of fresh vegetables, shiny apples, and long loaves of bread.

I watched fascinated while one man carefully, painstakingly, stacked his firewood so that it formed a lovely pattern while a large yellow cat stretched lazily in the warm sunshine beside him.

Window boxes lavishly filled with multi-colored flowers hung from the windows and balconies of each chalet. Their flaunting was almost gaudy, and caused me to wonder more than once, how the Swiss were able to exhibit such beautiful displays with seemingly little effort.

Leaving the shops and hotels of the village behind, we crept up the mountain cog by cog. At times we moved so slowly I thought surely we would soon start going backwards. We approached the top of the first rise and the little train seemed to give an audible sigh of relief as it paused in front of a small cafe to pick up a few more passengers.

A family dressed in t-shirts and shorts, sweaters wrapped around their waists, and comfortable hiking boots on their feet, hauled their backpacks into the train and took their seats beside us.

With a sudden jolt, the train continued, pulling us up, over, and around the steep mountainsides.

The scenery grew more splendid, the air cooler, and our anticipation greater as we rounded the last bend. In sight of our destination, the little train seemed to take courage and gathered speed before shuddering to a halt in front of the station.

Collecting our belongings we descended the steps and stood on the platform. I took a deep breath of fresh Alpine air, and looked around.

We were above the timberline, so only a few wind-blown evergreens hugged these hills. In springtime, these mountainsides are a frenzy of wild flowers. In winter they are filled with brightly dressed skiers, sweeping down their slopes. In summer, vacationers comb their various trails, seeking serenity and renewed strength. But now, in late September, we had them almost to ourselves.

I looked at the vertical path stretching before us . . . steep, with rocks protruding from all sides. Not many were choosing that course: one or two ardent hikers, a

couple of sturdy Swiss farmers, and one American family seeking adventure. The few others meandering around seemed more interested in the path leading down to the cozy cafe. I had to admit, I was tempted to join them.

Wrapping my jacket around my waist I took a deep breath and began the steep ascent.

I don't like hiking . . . especially uphill in the Alps. I never have. I prefer leisurely walks, or strolls along flat terrain.

It quickly became obvious just how physically out of shape I was. I began to complain inwardly (I was too proud to say anything audibly). I huffed and I puffed. I took giant steps, then tried baby steps. Pretending to look at the view, I sat and rested on a rock. But soon the others, who were making the climb seem much easier, were far ahead and I had to rush to catch up. I tried walking backwards, then sideways. Nothing helped make the trek any easier. I was hot and had a difficult time catching my breath. I slipped on stones along the trail and the bag I was carrying seemed to grow heavier and heavier.

Miserable, I peered up ahead. It seemed so far to the summit. I longed for someone to push or pull me along. I glanced back and was tempted to turn around. As the incline became steeper, the path became more difficult. I almost gave up. How nice it would be to just sit down here under this bush and wait for the others to come back.

But I had been to the top before and I knew what it was like. I longed to see the breathtaking panorama once again. So I plugged on, one step at a time.

A short time later, I stopped again to catch my breath and wipe my forehead. Glancing back down the path, I was surprised to discover I was making progress. I suddenly realized I was more than halfway there!

I began to chuckle. *How typical of me.* I so often dread the challenges in my life. I moan and groan. I worry and lose sleep. I procrastinate and even try to wiggle out of them. I often long to just sit down under a tree and let others, who seem to have an easier time tackling challenges, enjoy the summits. Yet when I look back at my life, I realize that I have met most of the challenges God has given me and each time I reach the summit of another one, I am awed and thrilled by the reward.

What a difference the encouragement of past victories can make.

I began to relax and enjoy the slow, steady pace I had set for myself. Pausing every now and then to rest, I would take time to enjoy all the beauty of the world around me. After a few minutes I began to climb again. Slowly, steadily, one step at a time.

As I placed one foot in front of the other, I thought of the little sign hanging in my kitchen:

Praise and Pray
and Peg Away

Suddenly I took one last step and stood on the summit of Roc D'Orsay. The view was even more awesome than I had remembered. As far as the eye could see a panorama of snow covered Alps shimmered in the bright sunlight.

My immediate reaction was thankfulness. I had accepted the challenge, triumphed over it, and was now delighting in the reward. How grateful I was I had not given in to the temptation to give up.

Lord, please help me tackle the uphill challenges in my life, as I have this mountain . . . faithfully . . . one step at a time. Grant me glimpses of the summit . . . of that day when I will stand in Your presence, basking in Your beauty and brilliance, and hearing Your dear voice saying, "Well done, good and faithful servant."

The Clearing

My loved one had a vineyard on a fertile hillside.
He dug it up and cleared it of stones
and planted it with the choicest vines
(Isaiah 5:1b-2a).

I t was still early. I sat at the dining room table
with a cup of hot coffee. Nothing tastes better then that first cup of fresh coffee in the morning!

Sitting in that particular spot brought back a legion of
warm memories. It was in this room, as a child, that I ate
most of my meals. I had grown up in this cozy little house,
and played outside in that very yard.

Nothing much had changed and yet . . . I recalled
everything being so much *larger.* The round dining room
table seemed to have dwindled, and the curved window
wasn't nearly so large as I remembered. The yard, too, had
diminished in size since I used to play dress up and pretend I was Mrs. Vanderbilt from Ft. Lauderdale, Florida.
My "mansion" had been located securely behind a hedge
of thick rhododendron bushes. (I never dreamed that one
day Ft. Lauderdale would actually be my home.)

A big thunderstorm had passed through the previous
night, drenching our cove with heavy rain. The little

stream rushed eagerly along as it tumbled over the tiny waterfall my mother had built years ago. A few raindrops still clung to the leaves of overhanging trees and each time the pesky little squirrel, who delighted in stealing the bird-seed, jumped from branch to branch, a shower of drops would accompany him.

As I looked out over the familiar yard, I suddenly noticed one major reason why it all seemed so much smaller. *It was.*

The yard of my childhood had been larger—literally. The trees, bushes, and surrounding undergrowth had continued to grow just as I had, and the yard had simply become overgrown.

I grabbed another cup of coffee and quickly went to put on my jeans. Grabbing a rake and a pair of clippers, I launched into my attack. It wasn't until several hours later, discouraged and thoroughly exhausted, that I had to admit the job was bigger than me. All my labors had hardly made a dent!

If the job were to get done, I needed some help.

Soon, my friends David and Greg arrived with tree-climbing boots, a chain saw, and a large chipper. I pointed out the problem and they began to work with a will.

The chain saw whined all day while I went back to my window to sit and watch.

David and Greg pruned, cut, pulled, dragged, sawed, and raked. Brambles, twisted vines, fallen trees, rotten stumps, weeds, undesirable saplings, leaves, and branches, were all removed. It wasn't long before an enormous mound of debris piled up in the middle of the driveway. Then, in just a matter of minutes, the chipper transformed it all into a mound of useful mulch to be spread around the flower beds.

Soon, I began to see a clearing in the dense undergrowth. The sun streamed in and the dampness lifted. The moldy smell began to dissipate and we discovered all sorts of treasures hidden beneath the debris: small holly trees, azalea bushes, and dogwoods. I stood amazed at the transformation.

After supper, I again sat at the picture window, drinking in the beauty. I watched squirrels leap from branch to branch in the large oaks, saw birds darting and flitting, and even caught a glimpse of a woodpecker working hard for his supper on the trunk of the maple. I noticed soft green moss climbing over the stones and up the stumps, observed a cluster of puffy mushrooms, and watched a mole enlarging his front porch. Winding through this scene, the merry little stream negotiated its way over and around the rocks. As the sun slipped lower in the sky, the slanting light played hide and seek in the branches, casting summer evening shadows along the edge of the grass.

Sitting there, I couldn't help thinking how much this yard reminded me of my life.

The overgrowth of activities and unnecessary busyness that allowed the boundaries of life to close in around me. . . .

The entangling brambles of bad habits, compulsive behavior, or unwise relationships. . . .

The rotten stumps and moldy leaves of unpleasant memories, unconfessed sin, or musty guilt hidden beneath the debris. . . .

The heavy, dead logs of burdens and problems that I try to lug around in my own strength. . . .

The undesirable saplings and undergrowth that seem so small and insignificant—like spending habits, TV programs, or reading material—yet could grow into serious problems if left unpruned and untrimmed.

The mildew of a complaining spirit or negative attitude that puts an unhealthy dampness on my disposition and dims the joy of those around me.

All of these things keep the positive, the worthy, the beautiful from growing. They choke, hide, and bury the deep beauty. They keep the Son from reaching much of my life and allow mold and musty unpleasantness to blight my heart and relationships.

I have often tried to clear the yard of my life alone. I've tried to chip away at the undesirable growth, remove a few of the boulders, or tear out some rotten stumps. But I soon grew weary and gave up. I had neither the will, the strength, nor the proper tools. But when I humbly called for help and allowed the Lord Jesus to weed, cut, and prune the undergrowth and debris, I have been amazed at the hidden beauty.

—A deeper relationship with the Gardener.

—A stronger sense of serenity and peace.

—A sharper focus on the important things in life, the things of eternal value.

Clearing, cutting, and pruning are not always pleasant. It is difficult, grueling, and at times heartbreaking work. If you find yourself overwhelmed at the prospect, drop me a line.

I can recommend a Gardener.

The Place of Refreshment

The warm air was heavy with dust. It blew in through the open windows of the mini-van, coating everything with a layer of grit. My once black T-shirt was rapidly turning gray.

Our driver seemed oblivious to the dust, noise, traffic, and ruts in the road. Horn blaring, he plowed through the streets at an amazing speed. Strangely, no one seemed the least perturbed . . . except Mother, my two sisters, and me.

We entered a village, passing a small girl with a long stick leading a gaggle of geese. As we slowed for a narrow bridge spanning a canal, we watched in fascination and horror as a woman washed her vegetables right next to another emptying her night soil and rinsing her honey pot in the same water. Beside them, a man was bent over the entrails of a long snake he was preparing to sell at the market while children splashed around their mothers washing clothes on rough stones.

We eased out of this village and into the countryside

bordering the Grand Canal of China. Cormorant fishermen floated by in their *sampans*, their birds standing beside them while long lines of barges jostled and pushed one another slowly up the canal. Water buffalo grazed lazily along the banks while others plowed nearby fields alongside old men in blue trousers and large straw hats.

Our minivan sped on. Every now and then, spying something of particular interest, one of us would yell, "Stop!" and our driver would brake to a sudden, screeching halt. We would descend from the van, causing quite a scene for those not used to Western women. Immediately a group of Chinese peasants would gather around us, curiously watching our every move.

After two days of dusty travel over roads and through villages where few, if any, foreign tourists venture, our van deposited us at the front door of a dingy government guest house in the town of Mother's birth.

We went to our rooms.

With the exception of the hot water contained in large thermoses, everything was dirty. The floor was spotted with spit, the curtains gray with grime, and the bed covers curiously stained. In the corners and under the furniture was a thick layer of dirt. The air was stale and we longed to open the windows, but the dust filtered in, only making it worse.

We went down to dinner. The small, drab, dining room reeked with the same mingled odors of cooking oil, liqueur, stale food, urine, and—whatever it was—that permeated every restaurant and guest house we visited. The stained white table cloth was covered with indecipherable dishes of various colors and consistencies, which we dared not examine too closely.

It was almost overwhelming, but we were determined to be polite. With much effort, we somehow managed to get

through the official welcoming banquet given by the mayor. We spent the next two days discovering more of our mother's heritage—including visits to the house where she was born and the homes of several of her old friends. Then we climbed back into the van and continued our dusty ride along the backroads of China.

Several bumpy hours later, we rolled through the outskirts of the large, much more modern city of Nanjing. Our van pulled up to the entrance of one of the nicer hotels. My mother, sisters, and I entered the lobby, greatly relieved by the absence of "the smell."

We went to our gracious, clean rooms and immediately called the valet to pick up our dust-covered clothes. Grabbing the room service menu we were elated by the fact that most of the items listed were recognizable. We then took turns bathing—in clean tubs where hot water flowed freely—while our food order was being prepared.

Later, clean and refreshed, we all sat around the table satisfying our hunger with hamburgers and french fries covered with ketchup. It tasted so good. As we sipped cold Cokes, we remarked to one another how wonderful it was to feel clean. How good to have our tummies filled and a comfortable bed to look forward to. It suddenly dawned upon us how like our Christian lives these last few days had been.

As believers, we daily face the spiritual poverty and moral filth of the world around us. We are forced to deal with situations and circumstances foreign to our spiritual nature, often having to endure the effects of the amoral fallout which descends upon us from every arena.

We spend our days with co-workers who constantly abuse our Lord's name or laugh at crude jokes. We sit next to someone at the hairdresser who wears an "I am Pro-Choice button." We take our children to a PG-rated movie

only to be shocked at the language and sexual innuendoes. We discover that one neighbor is cheating on his wife while another is cheating Uncle Sam. We are alarmed and discouraged by what our children are taught and exposed to in school and horrified at what comes into our homes by way of television, newspapers, and magazines.

We become tired of the rough roads and dirty environment. We feel soiled, experience spiritual hunger, and even become demoralized because of the effects of the sinful world around us.

However, like in the hotel in Nanjing, we can find cleansing, refreshment, and nourishment at any time, by simply entering the door of His presence. The dirt and dust that settles on our hearts and minds as we travel this world will be washed away by the pure water of Life, and we can experience continuous cleansing through the washing of the Word. Our spiritual hunger will be satisfied by the Bread of Life. In coming to Him, we discover rest for our souls. With David we sing,

> You have made known to me the path of life;
> you will fill me with joy in your presence,
> with eternal pleasures at your right hand
> (Psalm 16:11).

I turned out the light in Nanjing that night, then curled up in crisp, clean sheets with a prayer of thanksgiving on my lips for the cleansing, refreshing, nourishment, and much-needed rest.

Tomorrow I would be ready to face another day.

The Disappointment

We were worn out. We had gone from store to store circling miles out of our way to stop at yet another mall looking for a Teenage Mutant Ninja Turtle watch.

The first time six-year-old Antony had come home from school talking about Michelangelo, Leonardo, and the others, I thought, *Wow! I am really impressed by the teaching in kindergarten these days.* When I asked Antony more about these great artists, I was shocked by his reply.

"Mama," Antony replied with horror at my ignorance, "these are not painters—they're *turtles!*"

"Turtles!" I exclaimed with dismay.

That was my introduction to these characters and now we were searching all over the country because Antony had set his heart on a little plastic watch with a picture of a turtle on its face.

"Antony," his father said, "we will stop at one more store and if we don't find it we will have to give up for today."

We pulled into the K-Mart parking lot and Stephan took little Antony by the hand inside the store.

As they were going up one aisle and down another, Antony became more and more intense and suggested to his father that they not talk, but really "concentrate" on locating this object.

Soon it became evident that this store, too, was out of stock. Stephan became concerned over the anticipated disappointment from Antony.

"Antony . . . I don't want you to be too disappointed if we don't find a watch."

"Oh Dad," Antony replied looking up at his father with big blue eyes, "I won't be too disappointed about the watch. But I will tell you what I would *really* be disappointed about."

"Oh? What's that?"

"Now Dad," continued little Antony—who is rather theatrical, "what would *really* disappoint me, would be after all of the hard work we have done reading the Bible and praying, to find out that there is no God."

Stephan was stunned. *Well Antony*, he thought, *you wouldn't be the only one!* As a psychologist, Stephan has been trained and prepared for almost any emotional reaction. But he certainly hadn't anticipated this.

Later, as Stephan was relating the story to me, and we were laughing together, I found myself wondering. *What would make a six-year-old boy walking through K-Mart think of disappointment in the existence of God?*

As I was tucking Antony into bed that night, he asked, "Mama, how do we know there is a God? Just what if . . . *what if* there is no God?"

I leaned down and kissed him, assuring him he need

not worry, that there was a God and that this God loved him very much, just as I did.

I left the room feeling dissatisfied and frustrated. I felt so inadequate in my response. What could I say or do that would assure this little boy?

Although many years ago, I had accepted by faith the existence of God, the gift of salvation by grace through the death and resurrection of Jesus Christ, how could I explain faith to this young child? How could I convince him that he need never fear this particular disappointment again?

I thought back to my own childhood. I couldn't remember a time when I didn't believe in a living, loving God (even though at times I had my questions and doubts). How did my family teach and assure me of the existence and love of God? What did my parents do?

I thought of their example. God was such a reality to them He became a reality to me, too. Their faith was an everyday, all-day-long lifestyle, not something they slipped into on Sunday morning. They talked to and about God as though He was their best friend. They were so convinced He cared for them in a very personal way, that I grew up convinced He also cared for me. While still a young girl, I realized the Lord Jesus had become my best friend.

I remember my mother once reminding me that the best way to make a child eat his food is to let him see his parents enjoying theirs. I observed my parents and my grandparents taking delight in their faith. So I grew up enjoying rather than "enduring" my Christian life.

How important that example had been to me. How true that what we are speaks louder than what we say.

Was this part of Antony's problem? Was he seeing the reality of God's love . . . in me? Oh, he saw me reading the Bible

and praying. He knew I related everything to my faith and walk with Christ. But did I communicate to him just how precious and vital my faith was to me? Was my Christian walk causing this child to stumble or to seek more than what he saw in me?

Those thoughts forced me to my knees. I humbly asked the Lord to help me be a better example to my children so that they would "hunger and thirst after righteousness." Then the Lord brought to my mind His own simple, practical instructions on how to teach our children to love Him with all of their heart, mind, and soul.

Deuteronomy 6:5-8 tells us the process must begin with us moms and dads. The love of God must be a personal reality to us before we can pass it on to our children. Teaching our children, really, has to be an *overflow* of all that is in our own hearts. If our hearts are filled with the love of God, then we will find ourselves teaching and sharing with our children while we are walking or driving, at mealtime around the table, as we tuck them into bed at night or greet them in the morning.

In other words, it will be natural. It will become our very lifestyle.

By our examples, and the natural sharing that overflows from a full heart, our children will see that our faith is personal, vital, and real. Then, they too will come to know the reality of a personal, living God who loves and cares for them even more than we do.

A few days later we located the little watch.

"See Mama?" said Antony. "I prayed and God answered my prayer."

Are You Free?

It is for freedom that Christ has set us free.
Stand firm, then, and do not let yourselves be
burdened again by a yoke of slavery
(Galatians 5:1).

"Thereare two people in this world who make me nervous," said Basyle at dinner one evening, "and their names are Mama and Dada."

Then he went on to announce his plans of leaving home.

Not having any idea what had inspired this outburst from our young son, we were a little surprised. But Berdjette, his six-year-old sister, was shocked.

"*Basyle!*" she said indignantly. "That is what you call divorce! You are divorcing your father and mother!"

This information did not deter Basyle at all. He asked the babysitter to help him pack. If he moved in with the neighbors, he reasoned, he would be allowed to do as he pleased. To this four-year-old, leaving his parents and changing his environment meant freedom. Needless to say, he didn't get very far!

I chuckled to myself as I tucked him into his own little

bed that night. I couldn't help thinking that a lot of adults are guilty of the same false hope. They, too, believe that running away or changing their circumstances will produce freedom.

What they fail to understand, apparently, is that they cannot run away from themselves.

It is virtually impossible to experience freedom if one is encumbered by sin and guilt, or burdened by failure and dissatisfaction. We have to experience release from all that has been. Though we cannot undo what has been done or erase all the scars or turn back the years, we can encounter and receive God's forgiveness and healing through Jesus Christ, knowing that "if the Son sets [us] free, [we] will be free indeed" (John 8:36).

But we also need freedom within our present circumstances. We need to be liberated from our endless searching, from our griping and discontent, from constant worry and anxiety, from boredom and the barrenness of busyness. This is a liberation experienced only when we are no longer controlled by ourselves or our desires and compulsions, but by the Holy Spirit.

If we have accepted God's forgiveness and have been released from the burdens of the past, and if the Holy Spirit is controlling our present, then we will be free to face the future unafraid, knowing that God is already there. We will be free to do and be all that God intended. If we are liberated from ourselves, then we will be free to minister to others, to glorify God, and to enjoy Him forever.

It is through a totally dedicated heart that we experience true liberation.

Help, Lord!
I Need Strength!

For when I am weak, then I am strong
(2 Corinthians 12:10).

The massive jet lifted off the ground, making the familiar landmarks visible for only a few moments before its nose pierced the billowy white clouds and leveled off in the clear blue atmosphere. Outside my window, all was quiet, calm, and peaceful—so unlike the way I felt inside.

Depleted in both body and spirit, I was grateful no one was sitting in the seat beside me. I needed this time to be alone. Closing my eyes, I leaned back against the seat, longing for a moment of rest. But my mind continued to whirl like a cheap carnival ride. Flying high above the earth that day, I wished with David that these powerful wings would take me away where I could be at rest (Psalm 55:6).

With my eyes still closed, I listened to the drone of the engines, thinking about another weary woman who, some years before, had discovered her Source of strength. Mrs. Jonathan Goforth experienced heavy pressures and responsibilities as a busy wife, mother, and missionary to China. One day, finding herself overburdened and her strength insufficient, she turned to the scriptures. She was surprised and overjoyed to find that even the weakest may fulfill the conditions for receiving strength. What were those "conditions" of God's Word?

1. *Weakness*: 2 Corinthians 12:9,10
2. *No might*: Isaiah 40:29
3. *Sitting still*: Isaiah 30:7 (KJV)
4. *Waiting on God*: Isaiah 40:31
5. *Quietness*: Isaiah 30:15
6. *Confidence*: Isaiah 30:15
7. *Joy in the Lord*: Nehemiah 8:10
8. *Poor*: Isaiah 25:4
9. *Needy*: Isaiah 25:4
10. *Abiding in Christ*: Philippians 4:13

As I sat there, thinking and silently praying, I realized I had only fulfilled a couple of these conditions. I had not been sitting still and waiting, but running here and there, trusting in myself instead of placing my confidence in Him. I had not been waiting on the Lord in an atmosphere of quietness, but in a state of tension and anxiety until, once again, I had all but lost the joy of the Lord.

As the plane began its descent, I felt strangely warmed and renewed. My inner spirit began to sing:

Praise be to the LORD,
>for he has heard my cry for mercy.
The LORD is my strength and my shield;
>my heart trusts in him, and I am helped.
My heart leaps for joy
>and I will give thanks to him in song
>>(Psalm 28:6-7).

Conclusion:

There Is a Lifting Up

I opened the heavy wooded shutters only to discover that our chalet was shrouded in fog.

I went to the kitchen. Perhaps a cup of hot *cafe au lait* would help perk up my spirits. While I waited for the coffee to brew, I cut thick slices of bread for the children and set them on the table along with their grandmother's special milk jam.

Pouring a cup of the strong coffee, I went to get dressed for church. As I pulled a warm sweater over my head, I realized that for some reason I felt discouraged . . . even a little depressed.

Nothing particular had transpired to make me feel down. I just was. Because music often lifts my spirits, it crossed my mind to call the church and request one of my favorite hymns. I decided against it. Instead, I prayed.

Lord, I need a little lifting up today, and I have a special request. Could You please have the soloist at church sing "Unto the Hills" during the church service this morning?

I opened my bedroom door and going to the foot of the stairs, called out to the children to make sure they too were getting dressed. Soon they all tumbled down into the kitchen to grab their bread and jam.

As I passed the living room window, I noticed the fog was lifting. The sun was not far away and I was sure it would not be long before it burned off the remaining whiteness.

I hurriedly finished getting the children dressed, combing hair, washing off the remaining evidence of breakfast, and bundling each one up in coats and hats.

By the time we were all out the door and piled into the car, the sun was already breaking through.

It was early spring, and the Alps were still covered in snow. Although the air this time of year was still cool, the sun could be warm. I knew it would only be a few weeks before the mountainsides would exchange their thick blanket of snow for a colorful patchwork of wildflowers.

We headed down the mountain to the small, usually crowded chalet that served as a worship center.

We left our car parked a bit precariously on the edge of the narrow road, and I instructed the children once again to behave or else! We were fortunate to find enough empty chairs and I even got a seat next to the window which overlooked the steep narrow valley that separated us from the snow-covered mountains beyond.

By now, the fog had vanished altogether, and the brilliance of the sun reflecting off of the snow made the view even more breathtaking. Although Switzerland was home, I never got used to the magnificence of the mountains or the spectacular scenery which surrounded us. The steep, well-tended hillsides covered with lush vineyards; the sloping fields where large, lazy cows contentedly chewed their cud; the gentle Jura Mountains surrounding clean,

organized cities; the deep blue of the lakes dotted with boats of various sizes.

To me, all gave evidence to the majesty of God.

I had no reason to be despondent. I longed for the fog in my heart to lift just as it had on the mountainsides around me. My reverie was interrupted by the children who were already beginning to squirm. Oh, how I hoped they would sit still through the service—it was usually on the lengthy side.

The organ began to play the chords of the first hymn, which was followed by prayer and Scripture reading.

Then, the soloist stood to sing.

"Unto the hills around do I lift up my longing eyes," her deep melodious voice sang forth.

I couldn't believe my ears. How had she known? I had expressed my desire to no one except the Lord earlier that morning. Tears quickly filled my eyes.

Oh Lord, I gratefully and humbly cried, *thank You for this lifting up. For this brief but very personal moment of tender encouragement.*

Just as Jesus had taken Peter's mother-in-law by the hand and had lifted her up, so had He taken me by the heart and had lifted the fog from my soul.

I don't remember the rest of the service. I don't recall the message or if the children behaved or not. I don't remember what we ate for lunch or if we went for a walk that afternoon.

Yet even after all these years, I vividly remember the beauty of that Sunday and the special blessing of this personal, encouraging encounter with the Lord.

He is truly the lifter of my head.

Rapha

Gigi Graham Tchividjian has a deep concern for hurting people. Because of this concern, she serves as the National Advisor for Women's Affairs to Rapha Hospital Treatment Centers.

Rapha is caring for people . . . people of all ages and walks of life who have experienced the pain of mental disorders, emotional suffering, and substance abuse. Whether it's depression, substance abuse, eating disorders, suicidal tendencies, or other emotional problems, people need help in their hurting moments.

With twenty-three treatment centers located in hospitals from coast to coast, Rapha offers a full range of adult and adolescent care. Treatment programs offer a unique blend of clinical competence and biblical truth that lead to emotional and spiritual healing. In fact, the name Rapha is Hebrew and means "to heal." As a Hebrew name for God—Jehovah Rapha—it means "our God who heals."

If you or someone close to you is suffering

emotionally and needs help, call Rapha at 1-800-383-HOPE or 1-713-777-HOPE. A free assessment with a professional counselor is available. All inquiries are confidential and most insurance applies. For information about Rapha's books, videos, and other resources, or for information concerning Rapha's national network of support groups, call 1-800-383-HOPE or write:

> Rapha
> Hospital Treatment Centers
> 8876 Gulf Freeway, Suite 340
> Houston, Texas 77017